ORDINARY LIVES
EXTRAORDINARY
MISSION

FIVE STEPS TO WINNING
THE WAR WITHIN

JOHN R. WOOD

DynamicCatholic.com
Be Bold. Be Catholic.

ORDINARY LIVES
EXTRAORDINARY MISSION

ISBN 978-1-937509-31-6

Cover Design: Shawna Powell
Photo taken by Rick Perez (rniperez@gmail.com)
Internal Design: Shawna Powell

For more information on this title and other books and CDs
available through the Dynamic Catholic Book Program,
please visit: www.DynamicCatholic.com

The Dynamic Catholic Institute
2200 Arbor Tech Drive
Hebron, KY 41048
Phone 1−859−980−7900
Email info@DynamicCatholic.com

Printed in the United States of America.

TABLE OF CONTENTS

Prologue

Experience is the best teacher, but not the only teacher. We can learn from other people's successes, and we can learn from other people's failures. Wisdom is an acquired trait. Much of what is written in this book was generated from the wisdom of others. My intention in writing this book was not to create new ideas that have not yet been discovered. My intention was to share the lessons I have learned from the past and give you a guide to living those lessons. They are lessons from my own past, and lessons from the lives of heroes, legends, and saints who fill the history books.

I believe the lessons I am applying in this book are founded in truth. The great thing about objective truth is it applies to everybody, in every time, in every place, and in every culture. Truth is true for everyone, even people who don't believe in that truth. What I have come to discover is that truth lives inside each of us; it has been there from the very beginning. The ideas in this book are not unknown, but are perhaps forgotten by many people. A great teacher is not so much somebody who gives you information, but more so someone who helps you bring forth information. A great teacher doesn't give all the right answers; a great teacher asks all the right questions.

I don't have a theology degree and didn't even attend a Catholic high school. As an eye doctor, I have a secular career amid the secular world, and nowhere in my job description are the words "teaching the Catholic faith." Most people reading this book probably don't have that job description either. That is why I feel qualified to write this book. We are all teachers by the way we live and the people we become. Not having "Catholic careers" does not excuse us from being teachers of the faith. When others see how you live your life and your faith, you will bring forth great questions from them. Therefore, this book is a guide to living the Catholic faith in the job you do, the sports you play, the hobbies you enjoy, the families you raise, and in the way you influence people every day. You don't have to leave behind all the things of this world to put God first, but you must put God first in all the things of this world.

Much of the inspiration for this book came from great teachers who have brought forth the greatest questions from me. My Catholic education has come from great priests, authors, and speakers. A wealth of Catholic resources in this day and age is accessible to everyone. I owe a debt of gratitude to authors such as blessed John Paul II, Matthew Kelly, Scott Hahn, Jeff Cavins, Christopher West, and Peter Kreeft, to name just a few. Anyone familiar with these authors will come to see that I am their student. Many times as I am writing or preparing to speak to a group of people, I stumble upon a sudden realization, an idea that makes great sense. Later, when reading a book by John Paul II, Matthew Kelly, or some other great author, I come across the same idea written a different way. I begin to wonder, was this really my idea, or did I read about this long ago and forget having read it? Is it something I've heard before but forgotten? I have come to understand that these epiphanies are not my own—and Matthew Kelly, or John Paul II, or any other great author would probably agree. These ideas don't come from human beings—they come from God.

Truth does not need to be discovered; it just needs to be rediscovered. That truth is deep inside us and jolts us like déjà vu when we hear it. Perhaps it even scares us or makes us uncomfortable because we know it's true but we've been avoiding the truth since it requires change. We struggle with change, but this common objective truth unites us. We are all in this together.

Ultimately, our goal is the same. We each play the part of student and teacher. Somewhere along our journey, we are awakened by someone or something that inspires us, lights a fire inside, and gives us the gift of truth. And, like all great gifts, we can't just keep it to ourselves. It is not enough to hear the truth; we must take responsibility for it. We must take action. We must pass it on. We must pay it forward. For it is only in giving the gift away that it truly begins to bear fruit within us. My prayer is that this book will be that gift for you.

To Alan & Valeria

For my father, whose life provided me with a strong foundation and infinite opportunities, and whose death inspired me to make the most of those opportunities. In all my life's endeavors, I shall not forget you, or the promise I made the day we said good-bye.

Become Saints!

Introduction

In 1976 a young cardinal by the name of Karol Wojtyla was visiting the Unites States, and during his time here he said this: "We are now standing in the face of the greatest historical confrontation humanity has ever experienced. I do not think the wide circle of the American society or the wide circle of the Christian community realize this fully. We are now facing the final confrontation between the Church and the antichurch, between the Gospel and the antigospel, between Christ and the antichrist. This confrontation lies within the plans of divine Providence. It is, therefore, in God's plan, and it must be a trial which the Church must take up, and face courageously."[1] Two years later that man went on to become Pope John Paul II.

I don't believe the confrontation he spoke of is in some distant battlefield overseas or even in the culture around us. The problem is not out there. The greatest battle lies within, because this war takes place inside the human heart. John Paul II was a key member of the Second Vatican Council of the 1960s. Look closely at the message of this most recent Church council, which is not about an old Church changing on the outside, as many believe. The message of Vatican II is for us to change on the inside. One major theme in the documents is the universal call to holiness. The Catholic Church wants everyone to understand that it is not just priests and nuns who are called to be holy; we are all called to be holy. Holiness is a choice. The struggle to become holy is an internal war. Yet looking at our Church and nation today, I can't help but think we are losing this war. There are a lot of empty pews and people just going through the motions in churches. There are health care and economic crises. There are a lot of people just trying to get by and survive. And a spirit of fear dominates.

Yet despite all that is troubling throughout our nation and Church, I still see hope. However, if we are to end this crisis, we must stop pointing fingers and looking out there for solutions. The problems—and the solutions—lie within, so we must have the courage to look within. To win the war within, we must have a battle strategy. Peter Kreeft, a popular Catholic author of many books, proposed that to win any war you must know you're in a war, know your enemy, and know what weapons and strategies can defeat that enemy. I would like to build on Dr. Kreeft's battle strategy by offering the following five steps for winning the war within and becoming the saint God created you to be:

1. Know You Are in a War
2. Know Your Enemy
3. Free Yourself
4. Have a Shield
5. Have a Sword

These five steps will be a guide to help you live your faith in your everyday life. Jesus once said, "While I am in the world, I am the light of the world." (John 9:5) Saint Paul said, "So we, though many, are one body in Christ." (Romans 12:5) This means we are the body of Christ, and as long as we are in the world, we are called to be the light of the world. It is time we start choosing to be the light.

STEP

1

Chapter One
KNOW YOU ARE IN A WAR

[Jesus:] "In the evening you say, 'Tomorrow will be fair, for the sky is red'; and, in the morning, 'Today will be stormy, for the sky is red and threatening.' You know how to judge the appearance of the sky, but you cannot judge the signs of the time." (Matthew 16:2–3)

It has become rather obvious that something is wrong. The United States of America and the Catholic Church are in crisis. The word crisis pops up everywhere: economic crisis; health care crisis; vocations crisis; sex abuse crisis . . . the list goes on and on. However, these crises are not the root of the problem. The real problem is an identity crisis: As a nation and as a Church, we've forgotten our story and forgotten our mission. Central to knowing that you are in a war is knowing what you are fighting for and what you are defending. If you don't have a mission or a goal, then you won't see anything as a threat.

A DIVIDED CHURCH

As Catholics, we can't help but notice all the recent news articles and bad press about our Church. It is disheartening to read about sex abuse scandals, the decrease in vocations, empty pews, and young people walking away from the faith because they don't feel welcome. It is discouraging to hear that many Christians don't even consider Catholics to be Christians.

In college, I dated a wonderful young lady for several months. However, after learning I was Catholic, she seemed genuinely concerned and began to question my faith. Our relationship eventually ended because I am Catholic. Unfortunately, her perception of the Catholic Church was like that of countless other Christians. She saw Catholics as people who go through the motions, who don't have any real relationship with Jesus, who worship saints and Mary, who give too much power to Church authority, who abuse children, who don't welcome others at church, who drink way too much, and who give priests the power to forgive sins so people can sin as much as they want and then go to confession to wipe the slate clean. To her, Catholics focus on doing meaningless things to save themselves and don't believe they can be saved by faith alone. I must admit, her false perception was not all her fault. As Catholics we sometimes earn that reputation.

I don't think I've ever met a Christian who disagreed with Catholic teaching; I've only met Christians who have vastly misunderstood it. Their objections seem to be not with the supposed faults of the Church, but with the actual sins of her people. They misunderstand the faith because most Catholics neither live their faith nor, for that matter, even understand it themselves. In college, I remember meeting Christians of other denominations who seemed enthusiastic about God, but I felt hesitant mentioning I was Catholic. Subconsciously, I suppose, I feared what they would think of me, even though I personally love everything about my Catholic faith. I didn't like to admit to that fear, but it was there.

With more than one billion Catholics on the planet, many people are born into Catholic families.[2] They are Catholic by name and usually baptized Catholic as infants, but for many of them that's as far as they get. Most Catholics disagree with at least one aspect of their Church. They may identify themselves as Catholic and occasionally go through the rituals of Mass, but have little knowledge of the teachings of their faith. I must admit, I didn't know my faith well enough to allay that young lady's concerns. From what she perceived, Catholics don't belong in the category of "saved" Christians. However, I didn't have the right answers for her because I knew what I *did* as a Catholic, but I didn't know *why*. After our relationship ended, I went through a rough spiritual period with a lot of questions for God. I had nothing to do except search for truth. I believe God placed her in my life for a reason: to challenge me. She inadvertently led me to finding truth and, ironically, led me toward my wife, who has been instrumental in strengthening my own Catholic faith.

Up to that point, I had been a "good" Catholic, only because I was a good rule follower. But suddenly I didn't want to merely go through the motions anymore—I wanted to know *why*. I wanted my life to be an action, not a reaction. I also knew that it would do me no good to live by actions if those actions were not led by a guiding truth. This is dangerous territory, because many people stop following rules to be in control of their own lives and are led astray without the truth. My struggle continued through the summer after my first year in college, which was long and depressing. I felt like I didn't belong anywhere and the more I tried to do God's will, the more I was being punished. I felt alone and wanted answers.

My search for answers led me to an author by the name of Scott Hahn. A family member gave me a series of tapes in which

Hahn describes how he went from being an anti-Catholic Protestant minister to one of the most sought-after Catholic scholars and writers. His story brought me comfort that I was on the right path, and the more answers I sought, the more I found. And ultimately, the more answers I found, the more I fell in love with my Church and her beautiful history.

No matter what your faith is, it's my hope that this book will help you better understand the Catholic faith. To me, the similarities between Catholics and Protestants far outweigh our differences, although the differences are significant. Several Protestant friends have played a critical role in bringing me closer to God, and their genuine love of God inspires me. It is that genuine love of God and welcoming spirit I wish to bring to my Catholic friends and family. Sadly, it's the lack of genuineness and inability to engage others that have driven many people away from Catholicism. As Christians, we are all in this together, and our mission is the same: We all want to become who God wants us to become by embracing that relationship with our Savior and inviting countless others to do the same.

As Catholics, it is easy to get pulled into the masses of people going through the motions, especially if we are cradle Catholics (Catholic from birth). The Catholic faith is huge, and sometimes we let the vastness overwhelm us into believing that the truths of our faith are unattainable and unlivable. We need to understand that everything in the faith is there for a reason. As a Catholic priest once told me, the Catholic faith does not need anything added or taken away from it. It is like a treasure chest full of truth, established and given to us by Jesus Christ. The challenge is to unpack that truth and apply it to our own lives. This book is not about revealing new truths. Instead, it is a game plan for living the truth of the Catholic faith in the modern world in the

14

midst of our divided Church. Authentic lives will bring unity.

Despite what the American culture tells us, there is real truth, and that truth is possible to live out in today's world. In fact, the war we are fighting is precisely a battle between the real self and the false self. It is only when we start living with the arrogance that we can decide for ourselves what is right and wrong that we get into trouble. When man tries to make himself a god, he is waging war on the one true God. Fortunately for us, God made himself man to pay the price for our disobedience. We must choose to follow Christ's example and be obedient to the Father, trusting that he loves us.

A TROUBLED NATION

At this time in the United States of America, we can all agree that something is wrong; we just can't seem to agree on what it is. Finding the root of the problem and therefore finding the solution is a challenge. We know the economy took a severe dive, we know people have lost their jobs because of declining business, we know families continue to fall apart, and we know people have lost their homes to foreclosure. We have applied a Band-Aid to the problems for a quick fix, throwing money around where we feel it is needed. Quick fixes may cover up the problems for a while, but they will only return in larger form if we do not find the root of the problems and eradicate them. We treat the recent symptoms, but don't seem to realize the problems didn't start in the past couple of years.

Symptoms of a bad economy showed up recently, but the root of the problem has been there a long time. Our culture seems to promote more greed and self-centered need. We have become accustomed to getting what we want and more comfortable buying things we can't afford. We have confused needs with wants. We have bought into the cultural lie that says life is about what we do and what we have, so we have gone out to get what we want and done what we wanted to do without considering the consequences.

The U.S. health care system has severe problems, as well. We are spending more and more money but have less and less wellness. Some would argue we have continued to add years to our lives because of advances in technology, medication, and treatments. While we may have added years to life, we haven't necessarily added life to those years. The diseases keep coming, so we keep treating symptoms. Our health care system can't be fixed until we focus on treating the root of the problem, not just the symptoms. For example, depression in our young people has risen to epidemic levels over the past forty years. Sometimes depression is caused by a chemical imbalance in the brain that may require medication. However, it is not a virus causing this massive outbreak of depression in our country, but an underlying problem. A deeper problem is causing children to walk into classrooms and shoot their teachers, their classmates, and themselves. Ultimately, the crises we are experiencing are not bodily diseases, plummeting stocks, high taxes, or lack of jobs. No, these are just symptoms. The real crisis is an identity crisis.

THE PROBLEM AND SOLUTION WITHIN

The root of the problems for our country and for our Church is not out there, but lies within. We are at war. The war is internal and takes place inside the human heart—it is you against you.

Our nation is struggling because we are losing this war. Our Church is struggling because we are losing this war. Our families are struggling because we are losing this war. We can't find solutions by changing presidents and leaders, writing new laws, dumping money into the economy, bailing out businesses, changing medical insurance, or forcing people to follow government regulations. The attitudes of well-meaning people in our nation and Church seem to be attitudes of defeat. People make poor choices, and we have made poor choices ourselves. But instead of finding ways to help people choose to do good, we look for ways to justify our sins and the sins of others. We look for coping mechanisms for our sins. We try to justify our faults as if doing the right thing is simply not possible or "natural."

Communism and socialism are founded on the principle that people cannot choose for themselves. These political systems are run by dictators who rule with heavy hands. In America, we don't need a dictator to come and enslave us, because we have enslaved ourselves. The United States is the land of the free and the home of the brave, but if we don't start making better choices, we will soon be the land of the slaves and the home of the cowards.

GOD IS KING

Our nation and Church are founded on the same guiding principle that has made them strong for so many years: People are free to choose. And yet, we are only truly free inasmuch as we choose to do good. Our Church and nation have no human king. God is our king and we are "one nation under God." Freedom comes from God, but we are free only when we choose to follow God's plan, and God will never force us to do good. He may be king, but he is not a dictator. We have free will, so we choose our freedom, and we choose our slavery. As long as we continue to choose pride, envy, greed, anger, sloth, gluttony, and lust, we will be slaves.

Jesus tells us the war is within in the Gospel of Mark when he says:

> "Do you not realize that everything that goes into a person from outside cannot defile, since it enters not the heart but the stomach and passes out into the latrine? (Thus he declared all foods clean.) But what comes out of a person, that is what defiles. From within people, from their hearts, come evil thoughts, unchastity, theft, murder, adultery, greed, malice, deceit, licentiousness, envy, blasphemy, arrogance, folly. All these evils come from within and they defile." (Mark 7:18–23)

The war we fight takes place inside the human heart, and it is a battle of wills. No force on earth, and none in hell, can take our will from us. Our will is ours. We choose our happiness, and we choose our misery. Our Church and nation are being crippled by the same social diseases. If we are to have any hope of reviving them, we must focus on winning the war inside our hearts—the war between good and evil—and time is scarce.

MY MISSION

To see and understand the war going on around and inside us, it is vitally important that we understand our mission. The problem is that we have removed this mission from the culture. Remember, the crisis is an identity crisis, a crisis of saints. We have stopped telling young people to strive for perfection, to strive to be saints, because we don't want them to feel guilty about the times they fall short. However, the only way to say no to the cultural lies is to have a deeper yes. If you don't have something to fight for, then you won't see the cultural diseases as a threat. Do you know what you want out of life? Do you know what your goal is? Do you have a mission? What is your mission? These are all important questions you must answer.

What do you want for your life? I have personally reflected on this question extensively. After all, if you don't know where you're going, you're lost. To define clearly what it is that I want and don't want, I began to write down these things and memorize them. By clearly defining what I want, I can also clearly see what is a threat to my mission and rid my life of those things.

This is my mission:

I want my children's future to be better than their past. I don't want my children to worship pleasure; I want them to have pleasure in worship. I want to arm my children with the sword of truth so they have a fighting chance against an enemy that never sleeps. I want to be a better father and husband.

I don't want to go through the motions anymore. I want to help awaken the sleeping giant we call the Catholic Church. I don't want to ask "What's in it for me?" or "What's the least I can do?"

I want to master the virtues of justice, courage, wisdom, temperance, faith, hope, and love. I want to learn to love as God loves. I want Jesus to be proof that I can be a saint, and not to use him as permission to be a sinner. I want to learn to suffer well and carry the crosses of this life. I don't want to make excuses anymore. I don't want to say I'm too old, or too young, or don't have enough time, talent, or treasure—that is an insult to the one who gave me my time, talent, and treasure.

I want to be free, in the truest sense of the word. I don't want to be a slave to food, or drink, or any other possession of this world. I don't want my favorite sports team to determine what kind of mood I'm in anymore. I want to hear God's voice. I want to befriend silence. I want my life to be an action, not a reaction. I want to make a difference. I want my life to affect choices.

I want to fight the good fight. I want to finish the race with nothing left to give, because I do not want to face death and discover I have not lived. I want to see my father again and shake his hand, and know that he is proud of the man that I became. I want to be a saint with all my heart and inspire millions of others to do the same.

These are my dreams, but they are also my dreams for you. The details of our individual missions may vary, but the end goal is the same, to become the saints God created us to be. We must focus on this mission, understanding that anything not helping us accomplish it is, at the very best, a waste of time. Saint Paul says, "Finally, brothers, whatever is true, whatever is honorable, whatever is just, whatever is pure, whatever is lovely, whatever is gracious, if there is any excellence and if there is anything worthy of praise, think about these things." (Philippians 4:8)

Imagine how life would change if everything you did and said, everything you watched and listened to, everyone you were around, everywhere you went, everything you had and bought, everything you ate and drank, all was helping you become the saint that God created you to be. Now imagine the influence you would have on the people around you if all of this were true.

Most of us live divided lives. We are different people depending on the setting and who is around. If your friends and pastor were to have a conversation about you, would they think they were talking about the same person? Are you a different person during the week than on the weekends? Do you come home from work feeling as though you've been pretending to be somebody else all day to please customers or your employer? It is amazing how much other people influence our actions—and how much we influence theirs.

My mother comes from a strong Catholic family; she is one of eleven children. I am one of thirty grandchildren on my mother's side. Our family gatherings have always been quite large. My aunts, uncles, and cousins are wonderful people, and I'm impressed with what my mother and all ten of her siblings have accomplished in life, and the strong families they have raised. Yet even though I come from a large family, I've never felt comfortable at large family or social gatherings because of my shy, introverted personality. After graduating from high school, college, and optometry school, I gradually began to feel more confident around people. When my wife and I moved to a small town in northwest Ohio, where we barely knew anyone, it was like having a brand-new start in life. Nobody knew who I was, so nobody had any programmed expectations of me.

I began to take on several leadership roles in my church and as a doctor. I started coaching basketball, teaching class, giving talks at church functions, and speaking to nurses and staff at nursing homes where I see patients—all things my friends and family would never have expected because of my personality. (One of my aunts questioned my career choice because it involved talking to people.) I am still introverted and struggle at times with these leadership roles, but slowly I have become more comfortable in them. However, whenever I visit childhood friends and family, I find myself slipping back into the role of shy, unconfident kid. Growing up, I was always the younger cousin, little brother, and shy kid who didn't talk. During these homecomings I feel and act differently than I do as a father, husband, doctor, teacher, and coach in my current hometown.

We live divided lives because we react to different circumstances and situations. Wanting to be loved and accepted by others, we often react in ways we feel people want or expect us to. That often is why change is difficult. If a certain person has a reputation of being the life of the party, his friends are going to start expecting this from him. This reputation may cause this person to develop bad habits, such as drinking too much and smoking. Perhaps he realizes his habits are bad and would like to quit, but he has built his identity with friends around these habits. I have witnessed many people make great strides in becoming healthier and breaking free from bad habits; put them around the wrong people, though, and their progress is halted. This is why it is so important to know our goals and missions in life, and to make a list of things we do and do not want out of life. A clearly defined mission and clearly defined goals turn our lives from reactions into actions.

To become the saints we were created to be, we may need to avoid certain people at certain times. Spending time around others striving to become saints, who encourage us to have and do the things that will help us become saints, makes our goals much more attainable. This may be the first step—to retreat from the world for periods of time so we are not tempted to fall for the lies and deceit. Eventually we need to reach the point where we can focus solely on our missions no matter what the situation or circumstance. This deeper yes helps us say no to the lies and deceit, but it also gives us courage to help others on their journeys.

THEY WILL FOLLOW YOU

Discovering our mission, we realize we are not called to abandon the world and run from evil. Instead, the mission challenges us to live right in the middle of the world. However, by living in the middle of the world, we're tempted to focus on changing others and their faults to make us feel better about our own lives. We are tempted to judge others, to read stories in the Bible and wonder, "How can those people do such horrible things?" Those stories teach us about ourselves; every character acts as a mirror. Only God can read the hearts of individuals. We can't claim to know how others are struggling, or where each is on the journey. Are you so focused on others' faults that you can't see your own? If you readily see faults in others, I encourage searching within yourself—more often than not, you'll discover the same faults.

The reality is, to change others, we must change ourselves. Sometimes we must call out our loved ones and in charity explain how their actions are self-destructive. However, we can only do that when we are willing to change ourselves. Perhaps we can share our own struggles to help them see we all have weaknesses and together can overcome them. They may be willing to listen, or not. Ultimately, when we focus on changing ourselves for the better, it automatically challenges others to change as well. This is a difficult challenge, and Chapter 3 describes ways to free ourselves. That step cannot be accomplished until we accept that we are all prisoners to some degree. This book is about five steps to help you become a saint. It is not a book about five steps to help you become a nice person, or a good person. This challenge is a call to become something more, and it will be met with great resistance. It is a call to seek and find the narrow way.

Pride tells us nothing controls us, that we are free. We pretend vices and addictions don't hurt anything. We become defensive if somebody tries to imply that the things we love in this world prevent us from becoming saints and hold us captive. I encourage you to seek out your weaknesses, no matter how small the world perceives them, and crucify them. By doing so, you'll challenge people around you to do the same. Your friends and family may not like this challenge, but when you begin to become who you are meant to be, they will see a peace in your eyes for which they will long. True holiness is attractive. We must come to discover that a loving spouse, good parent, and true friend is one that helps us become a saint. These people are our greatest allies. If we want to surround ourselves with people who help us become saints, we must be a person who helps others become saints.

As parents, we spend much time worrying about how to lead our children down the right path. The best thing each of us can do for our children and family is to become a saint. The best thing each of us can do for our friends, coworkers, city, school, nation, Church, and the world is to become a saint. We reveal Christ to the world through ourselves. No, scratch that. Christ reveals himself to the world through us, if we allow him. We reveal Christ not only by things we do and say, but by who we become. Unfortunately, very few people are striving toward becoming who they were created to be.

EXCUSES, EXCUSES, EXCUSES

Many excuses can justify our failures. One is that nobody is perfect, which is true. This is ingrained in our minds from youth, and so we exploit and stretch the excuse for all we can. How many times have you heard the phrase "You can never be perfect"? That is a lie—a lie with good intentions, but still a lie. We focus on ways we are not perfect and believe the lie because we also falsely believe that life is about what you do and what you have. If that is true, then we can never be perfect. For example, making a free throw in basketball is not too difficult. However, on any given day, if I were to shoot a hundred free throws, chances are I might miss one (or maybe a few more than that). I am human and there are times when I lose my concentration and get tired. Does that mean I'm not perfect? It does if we're talking about what we do and what we have. Fortunately, life truly is not about what we do and what we have. Life is about who we become. Each of us was created for a specific purpose, and God has given us the potential to fulfill that purpose. Through Christ's death and resurrection, every person has the power to choose to become who he or she was created to be. I am a sinner, and I am not perfect. But I am perfectible.

CALLED TO PERFECTION

Christ didn't die on the cross just so our sins would be forgiven or to give us coping mechanisms for our sins. He came to give us the power to overcome sin, to free us from sin, and he is our model. John Paul II once said, "It is in the Gospel that the aspiration to perfection, to 'something more,' finds its explicit point of reference."[3] Christ calls us to something more: "So be perfect, just as your heavenly Father is perfect." (Matthew 5:48) He gives us the power to choose to be perfectly who we were created to be. Sin, by definition, is a conscious turning away from God. We can't sin accidentally—it is a choice. In any given moment, I can choose to turn away from God or I can choose to do the right thing. In choosing to do the right thing, I'm taking a step toward becoming perfectly who I was created to be.

We have overwhelmingly embraced the mantra "nobody's perfect" because it hides our fear. Americans, and many Christians, maybe now more than ever, live in fear. It's not a fear of external restraints that takes away our freedom. It is a fear of internal restraints that enslaves us.

I have to admit that fear was a dominant emotion for the first thirty years of my life. What was I so afraid of? I always thought I had a confidence problem. I was afraid of any trial or test, and even though everyone kept telling me, "You can do it," I thought the fear of failure was holding me back. Eventually I came to discover that my fear was not of failure, but of success. I didn't want to believe I "could do it" because that would hold me accountable. It is much easier to live life believing we are not capable of living the truth. However, to be credible witnesses to the power of the cross, we must confidently trust that God will make himself manifest through our lives. As Saint Paul says, "I have the strength for everything, through him who empowers me." (Phillipians 4:13)

For too long I have hidden behind the excuses of "I'm not perfect" and "This is just who I am; stop trying to change me." I am probably not the only one who struggles with these thoughts. But this is not who we are. We are children of God, sons and daughters of the most high, heirs to the Kingdom of Heaven, and we were born to be saints! As Christians, we often speak of glorifying God. However, we don't seem to realize the glory of God is the perfection of creation. We glorify him by becoming saints and inspiring others to do the same. If we continue to identify ourselves with our sins and refuse to believe we can change, then we strip the cross of its power.

Yes, we have the power to become saints—and the power to help others become saints. That is our goal, a mission that has been watered down by well-meaning people who thought the goal was too far-fetched and didn't want to risk a life of failure reaching for what they perceived was an impossible dream. However, eliminating the mission does not free us from burdens; it enslaves us in lives of quiet desperation, in which we are always

searching for meaning but never finding it. It is time we rediscover our mission, and take responsibility for the power we are
given. We are afraid of that power because it leaves no room for
excuses. It slaps us with the cold reality that we have chosen who
we've become as a nation, as a Church, and as people.

The good news is we have the power to choose who we become from here on out. We can change, and we must. Change
is about winning the war inside our hearts. Becoming a saint is
truly possible. There are many definitions, but simply put, a saint
is somebody who is perfectly who he or she was created to be,
somebody who is in heaven.

I assume everyone reading this book wants to go to heaven,
but think of this: God gave us free will because he wants us to
experience his love. He wants us to love as he loves, and one quality of God's love is that it must be free. This is why he will never
force us to do anything. For love to be love it must be free, so
God will never take away our free will. All of us, at some time,
use that free will to choose sin. But there is no sin in heaven.
Therefore, if there is no sin in heaven, and God never takes away
our free will, then somewhere along the line we must become
perfectly who we were created to be; we must choose to be saints.
This doesn't happen overnight. It takes a lifetime to make a saint.

Sometimes a lifetime is not long enough to make us saints.
The Catholic Church teaches that if we don't become fully who
we were created to be in this life, then we will need a final purification before we enter eternal glory. We call that final purification purgatory, which is a subject of disagreement between
Catholics and Protestants. C. S. Lewis, the great Christian writer,
once said:

> Of course I pray for the dead. The action is so spontane-
> ous, so all but inevitable, that only the most compulsive

theological case against it would deter me. And I hardly know how the rest of my prayers would survive if those for the dead were forbidden. At our age, the majority of those we love best are dead. What sort of intercourse with God could I have if what I love best were unmentionable to him? I believe in Purgatory.

Mind you, the Reformers had good reasons for throwing doubt on the "Romish doctrine concerning Purgatory" as that Romish doctrine had then become. . . .

The right view returns magnificently in Newman's dream. There, if I remember it rightly, the saved soul, at the very foot of the throne, begs to be taken away and cleansed. It cannot bear for a moment longer "With its darkness to affront that light." Religion has claimed Purgatory.

Our souls demand Purgatory, don't they? Would it not break the heart if God said to us, "It is true, my son, that your breath smells and your rags drip with mud and slime, but we are charitable here and no one will upbraid you with these things, nor draw away from you. Enter into the joy"? Should we not reply, "With submission, sir, and if there is no objection, I'd rather be cleaned first." "It may hurt, you know"—"Even so, sir."

I assume that the process of purification will normally involve suffering. Partly from tradition; partly because most real good that has been done me in this life has involved it. But I don't think the suffering is the purpose of the purgation. I can well believe that people neither much worse nor much better than I will suffer less than I or more. . . . The treatment given will be the one required, whether it hurts little or much.

My favorite image on this matter comes from the dentist's chair. I hope that when the tooth of life is drawn and I am "coming round," a voice will say, "Rinse your mouth out with this." This will be Purgatory. The rinsing may take longer than I can now imagine. The taste of this may be more fiery and astringent than my present sensibility could endure. But . . . it will [not] be disgusting and unhallowed. [4]

I love Lewis's point that we "demand purgatory." I once heard a theologian say we each choose our own sentence in purgatory when we see our own soul as it is and how it is capable of being. Purgatory is a cleansing, a final preparation for heaven. Whether we need a purgatory or not, the point is that we can become saints.

A saint is not necessarily somebody who skips purgatory. Saints, canonized and uncanonized, are the souls in heaven, and they come from every culture and background. The Catholic Church calls them the Church Triumphant. They are a diverse group of people with often very different paths, but the path to sainthood is well trodden. Many ordinary men and women have lived extraordinary lives. The mission seems far-fetched and difficult, which is perhaps why many people avoid the journey, or why those well-meaning people stopped encouraging others to be saints. We want instant results, and to tell somebody who has never run a race to go run a marathon tomorrow morning would certainly set them up for failure.

All great things are accomplished little by little. This mission of sainthood is accomplished one habit at a time. It takes perseverance, forgiveness, and courage to keep moving forward on the journey from where we are today, point A, to becoming the saint we were created to be, point B. The important thing is not to land on point B tomorrow, but to be closer to point B tomorrow than you are today. To run a marathon, you must train, and with training, you improve, little by little. With persistence, and our eyes fixed on our goal, we will eventually do what we never dreamed we could and, more important, become the person we never knew we could become—a saint. This is our goal, our mission, our deeper "yes" that gives us the motivation to say no to the many cultural influences, diseases, and lies that threaten this mission.

MISSION 1:

Applying the First Step to Winning the War Within

CONSTANT REMINDERS

It is not that difficult to realize we have a war waging within. It is not even too difficult to become inspired or to discover our mission. A song, movie, speech, or experience can spark a fire inside. The difficulty is in staying inspired to live the mission; to turn the spark into a raging fire that can't be extinguished. The real world is full of distractions, but it is precisely in the midst of distractions and the real world that we are called to live the mission. To do so, we need reminders to hold us accountable for what we are trying to accomplish. This mission must be on our minds every waking hour of every day.

A great piece of wisdom from the author Matthew Kelly is to create and post constant reminders of the goal. I taped the phrase "Become a Saint" to my alarm clock so it is the first thing I see when I wake up in the morning. Then I taped it to my bathroom mirror, the dashboard of my car, and my computer. I make it the screensaver on the computers I work on all day. I wear a wristband with these words so I see it every time I look at my watch. Why? I want to be reminded of my goal constantly. I want it staring me in the face when I make decisions throughout the day. Many spiritual demons have a mission to prevent you, and as many souls as possible, from reaching your goals. Saving souls is worth the fight.

Your challenge to live out Step 1 of winning the war within is to post constant reminders to hold yourself accountable for living the mission. Put the phrase "Become a Saint" on your television, radio, refrigerator, computer, and everywhere you are fighting the war, so you can constantly ask yourself, "Is what I am about to do helping me accomplish my mission?" You will be amazed how powerful this exercise is. Not only will it help you keep your focus on your mission; it will spark the interest of others who see it, and you will have the opportunity to explain it to them. With this great mission to become a saint clearly in mind, you will be able to open your heart and see the battle raging inside.

STEP
2

Chapter Two
KNOW YOUR ENEMY

Your opponent the devil is prowling around like a roaring lion look-ing for [someone] to devour. Resist him, steadfast in faith, knowing that your fellow believers throughout the world undergo the same sufferings. (1 Peter: 5:8-9)

Have you ever listened to professional football players and their coaches talk about how they prepare for games? They watch a lot of game film of themselves because they want to know their own weaknesses and fix them. The greatest battle lies within, and you begin to arm yourself by knowing yourself. The path toward perfection revolves around finding your weaknesses and chang-ing them into strengths.

Besides watching films of themselves, coaches and players also watch films of opponents. Why? To know everything they can about their opponents. They want to know exactly how many times they run each play; what they do against certain defenses; how often they tend to blitz; how they react when they get ahead or behind; what kind of plays they run; where the quarterback likes to throw the ball and how long he takes to throw it. They study their opponents inside and out because the better they know their opponents, the more likely they are to defeat them.

THE GENIUS OF SATAN

There is a great opponent in this war within. There are dark forces trying to prevent us from winning the war, and Satan is extremely intelligent. The legend goes that he was the most intelligent of all the angels—so intelligent that his pride got the best of him and he thought he was better than God.

If we're to have any chance of winning this war, we must understand the tactics of the dark side. The genius of Satan is that he has convinced most of the world that he doesn't exist. An October 2002 study by Barna Group ("Americans Draw Theological Beliefs From Diverse Points of View") found that 59 percent of Americans reject the existence of Satan, instead believing he is merely a symbol of evil. The study states, "Catholics are much more likely than Protestants to hold this view—75% compared to 55%—although a majority of both groups concur that Satan is symbolic." The religious group with the highest percentage (59 percent) of members who believe that Satan is a living entity was Mormon. The group with the lowest percentage, at 17 percent, was Catholic.[5] This is a problem, because to defeat our enemy, we must first believe in our enemy.

Satan's mission is to steal souls, and as with any thief, it's much easier to steal something when nobody knows you're there. Imagining Satan as a big red devil with large black horns, we figure that if he does exist we'll know him when we see him. However, as I mentioned, Satan is no dummy. He won't come knocking on your door and say, "Hi, my name is Satan, would you like to join me in hell?" No, he works in much more subtle ways, using temptation, deception, and societal diseases to enslave and prevent us from making the journey toward sainthood.

There are three societal diseases in particular that Satan employs to destroy us. They have devastated our economy, health care system, families, businesses, nation, and Church. These diseases are scary because they work like cancer, starting deep within and quietly spreading. Cancer is so frightening because often by the time the symptoms of the disease start to show up, it may be well advanced. At the same time, these diseases operate like a virus, spreading from person to person, highly contagious.

Hedonism, individualism, and minimalism have cost our nation more money and more problems than heart disease, cancer, flu, and diabetes combined. Matthew Kelly first brought these societal diseases to my attention in his book *Rediscovering Catholicism*. Since then, I look back at the stages of my life and see their presence everywhere, in my own life and in the culture. In fact, American culture is saturated with these societal diseases. Not a day goes by that we don't see traces of their ugly faces. Understanding these three weapons of the enemy is essential to accomplishing our mission of becoming saints, so I will refer to them often throughout this book.

Signs of these diseases have rapidly shown up in our nation during the past several years, but they have been around for a long time. We have all been predisposed to these diseases since the Garden of Eden, and they are fatal to our souls. Like cancer, they've slowly eaten away at the morality inside each person; like a virus, they've spread rapidly from person to person.

When my father was diagnosed with liver cancer, we were confused because just weeks earlier his liver enzymes had been tested and found to be normal. The doctor told us the liver can function normally with up to ninety percent of it destroyed. By the time symptoms start showing up, the cancer is advanced. It may not be too late for our culture, but we must act quickly.

So what are these societal diseases, and how do they work? Before we look at the "game film" of the opponent, let's get familiar with the individual players—hedonism, individualism, and minimalism—on the other team and see how Satan has successfully implemented them in our culture.

HEDONISM

Hedonism is the motto "If it feels good, do it." This attitude comes from the destruction of self-discipline. Hedonism is the primary culprit of the health care crisis and the sex abuse crisis. Hedonism is why pornography has become a multibillion-dollar business, making more money than professional football, baseball, and basketball combined. Hedonism is why sexually transmitted diseases are running rampant. Hedonism is promoted by our culture as a path to happiness; that is why every other television commercial displays a big, juicy hamburger or a beautiful woman who is only half-dressed, attaching pleasure to their products. Hedonism is derived from the deadly sins of gluttony and lust.

The difficulty in confronting this opponent is that we rarely feel like doing the things we should to keep us healthy and happy. I love my job, but I rarely felt like taking exams or going to class, especially for eight years of college. I love being healthy, but I rarely feel like exercising. I have always loved playing sports, but rarely felt like going to practice. I love knowing things, but rarely feel like studying. I love my children, but rarely feel like playing tea party or changing diapers.

With all its might, our culture screams the hedonistic philosophy at young people, promising a life of happiness if you can just do what feels good. That culture has convinced us that pleasure and happiness are the same thing, which is a dangerous lie.

My wife is a healthier eater than I, and she simply does not like fast food. Since I've been married, I've very rarely had fast food, and can probably count on one hand the times my children have had it. Recently, though, they brought home a box of fast food chicken nuggets. On the front of the box it stated, "An excellent source of happiness." Most food labels attract customers by claiming it's an excellent source of vitamin A or C, omega-3, or some other nutritious ingredient. Obviously, chicken nuggets have little to no nutritional value, so the marketing geniuses came up with the line "An excellent source of happiness." I believe they're confused. Perhaps it is an excellent source of pleasure, but not happiness. Pleasure is fleeting. As soon as the nuggets are gone, no more pleasure. Unlike pleasure, happiness can be sustained long after the event that causes it. Yet we think we'll be happy if we can just get enough pleasure.

In a hedonistic culture, pleasure becomes the ultimate goal. This is why well-meaning parents tell their children, "If you don't feel like doing it, don't do it," or, "If you are not having fun then just quit," or, "The most important thing is that you have fun." After coaching high school basketball players for four years, I can see the flaws in this mentality. A high school boy's idea of fun is seeing how many full-court shots he can make, or scrimmaging Harlem Globetrotter–style. There is nothing wrong with fun, and it is important, but it is dangerous to say fun is the most important thing. Playing tough defense, running sprints to get in shape, coming to practice every day, and diving for loose balls aren't always fun. However, these things make a great basketball player. They may not be fun in the short term, but in the long term they help you increase your abilities and win games, which *is* fun.

Remember, though, that winning is not the most important thing either. Losing is not fun, but even if we put our heart and soul into something and lose on the scoreboard, we still accomplish our mission of becoming all we can be. The scoreboard is important only in that it inspires us to accomplish the mission of doing our best. "Leave it all on the floor" was a common saying I used with my players—to give everything you have and not do things halfheartedly. Do your best and let God do the rest. That is the most important thing.

Living in a constant search for pleasure has not brought happiness but a life of a thousand addictions. American youth have grown up in an environment in which they have seemingly had opportunities to do and have more than ever before. Yet the amount of medication prescribed for depression seems overwhelming, and it is heartbreaking to read news stories about suicide, which is the third leading cause of death in young people age fifteen to twenty-four. [6] Everyone has addictions or vices, some big and some small, which tells us that our bodies make wonderful servants but horrible masters—much like money.

When we are hungry, our stomach growls. When we are tired, our eyelids get heavy. When we need to go to the restroom, our body informs us. When we're hot, we sweat. When we're sick, our body tells us to slow down. When we're hurt, we feel pain telling us something is wrong. The way the body works is genius. In a medical profession, all I've learned about the human body, especially the eye, points to an intelligent creator.

The human body's ability to give us and tell us what we need is unfathomable. However, in a society that's overindulged, the body not only tells us our legitimate needs; it also whines for illegitimate wants. The body doesn't just say, "I'm hungry"; it cries out, "I'm hungry for a double cheeseburger with cheesy fries and a large cola." The body has cravings, and when those cravings emerge, we give in to them as if we're prisoners. Sadly, we've stopped listening to our bodies when they tell us what we need. Instead, we've become their servants when they make demands. We often can't say no to the pleasures of eating, drinking, smoking, sex, gambling, drugs, and many other vices. No matter how big or small our addictions are, they all break our will.

The U.S. health care crisis and rising levels of diabetes, high blood pressure, high cholesterol, and heart disease illustrate that we're not fueling our bodies properly, and the fact that we're a "fast food nation" doesn't help either. Our overall reaction to these epidemics is disappointing. Most people will go to the doctor, find out they have one or more of these problems, and demand a pill. They may try diet and exercise for a short while, but realizing the discipline and work involved, they often will go back to the pills. The amount of drugs prescribed in this nation is overwhelming. Our bodies are telling us we need to change our lifestyles, but we don't want to, so we try to treat the symptoms with pills in order to continue doing what feels good.

A primary care physician told me it is easier to convince his patients to go to the drugstore and buy five hundred dollars' worth of drugs than it is to convince them they don't need any medication. We perceive drugs as if they're always good for us, when in fact this is rarely so. I have known friends and family members who take some kind of over the counter painkiller every day, often much more than the recommended dosage. Why do people take these pills so often? They will say that if they don't, they get a headache or continue to have a headache. The body tells them something is wrong, yet they think it isn't functioning correctly, so they take a pill to silence its cry for help. Sometimes pills are necessary, but more often than not we take them to avoid facing the root of the problem, which may require us to change our habits.

In many cases, the best treatment for an illness in a person with a healthy immune system is to let the body do its job and to assist with proper rest and nutrition, especially when it comes to viruses. However, when we don't feel well, we see it as a horrible injustice, and we want something to be done about it now. This attitude comes in part from our culture's mentality of avoiding suffering at all costs. We don't accept that suffering is unavoidable in this life (which we will discuss in greater detail later). We want control, and we see drugs as control, as an opportunity to free ourselves from changing anything. Ironically, if we don't change, we are not free—we remain slaves. When we make our daily choices based on how we feel, we rarely choose to do what is best for us. When I deny myself temporary pleasures of life in favor of disciplined efforts to better myself, the long-term effects are that I feel happier, healthier, and more passionate about life. We know the things that are good for us, but we've bought into the lie that pleasure equals happiness.

It is my hope and prayer that my children will not worship pleasure as the world does. Instead, I hope and pray they'll experience pleasure in worship and serving, understanding that pleasure makes us happy only when the activity producing it helps us to become the saints we were created to be. I hope and pray they'll be free in the truest sense of the word. To become the saints we were created to be, we must be free. Hedonism enslaves us and is a huge obstacle in making the journey toward sainthood.

INDIVIDUALISM

As human beings we are created to love and be loved. In contrast, things are made to be used. There is a great problem with a culture that loves things and uses people, but that's the trap into which we've fallen. It comes from this philosophy of "What's in it for me?" Individualism is why we have an economic crisis, and it has contributed to the health care crisis and vocations crisis. Individualism is derived from the deadly sins of pride (putting your will ahead of God's), anger, envy, and greed. The culture is proposing individualism as a path to happiness, and that is why every other commercial is trying to sell a product you must have to be happy. It is like the car salesman who says, "No credit? Bad credit? No problem! You come on down and we'll get you financed. You live in America; you deserve this car. Life, liberty, and the pursuit of *happiness*."

The culture promises that getting what we want will make us happy and successful, but how successful is a basketball team if each player is constantly asking, "What's in it for me?" How successful is a marriage if both people are constantly asking this question? Or a business, if the employees are constantly asking this question? How successful will parents be if they wake up every morning and ask, "What is my reward for being a parent?"

Becoming the saints we were created to be is about realizing that we are meant to serve. Just as the culture's lure of happiness through pleasure has not panned out, the promise of happiness through getting what you want has not panned out either. The philosophy of "What's in it for me?" contributes to the high rates of depression and teen suicide. Many people get what they want and yet remain unsatisfied and depressed. I believe many young people are lost because they have never learned to serve; they're constantly focused on their own desires. They haven't felt the pure peace and liberation of making a difference in someone else's life. Or if they have, it's far too seldom.

So many people are caught up in a vicious cycle of self-loathing. We are always victims of circumstance, and life hardly seems fair when it's focused on self. We are never satisfied, because we can never get enough of the things we don't need. This individualistic disease is programmed into us from a very early age. Although children have a genuine concern for others, they also possess a "me, me, me" attitude from the very start.

With my four small children, it feels like an endless task of teaching them to share. Christmas is a wonderful opportunity to stress the message of giving and not receiving, but everybody knows that a child wants to see a lot of presents with his name on them. My wife has always gone to great lengths to assure everything is "fair" with our children, even when they were babies. Each child receives the same number of gifts of equal value. No matter how hard she tries, there's always some degree of the grass being greener on the other side. You always hear things like, "How come she got a cat? I didn't get a cat."

Life will always seem unfair when we're focused on the wrong things, namely ourselves. We all have unique gifts and talents given to us by our creator for a specific purpose. That purpose is most certainly not to collect the most toys and self-indulge. These gifts are meant to serve others. In nature, every plant and animal has unique characteristics that help them survive in their particular environments. Albert Einstein once said, "Everybody is a genius, but if you judge a fish by its ability to climb a tree, it will spend its whole life believing it is stupid." A fish does not try to climb trees because it was not created to climb trees. Climbing trees is not essential to a fish's survival.

As human beings, we were created not to merely survive, but to thrive. We can thrive only when we use our unique characteristics in accord with their nature. Trying to serve ourselves is no different than a fish trying to climb a tree. It leaves us just as frustrated because we aren't designed to serve ourselves. We are designed to serve others.

A few years ago, one of the many problems with our house was a strange mold growing in the window sill of our daughters' bedroom and the bathroom. I kept spraying it with chemicals, but it kept coming back. Eventually, I got worried it may be detrimental to our health, so I called a mold inspector. He tested for moisture, but wasn't detecting much in the wall and recommended that I keep spraying the mold. But the mold kept coming. I finally decided to tear out the whole wall and discovered the wood studs underneath were so soaked they were crumbling to the ground like mush. Soon after, we pinpointed the problem: The windows had been installed incorrectly. The window ledge on the outside of the house was slanted inward, causing water to sit on the window ledge until the seal broke and water came in relentlessly over the years. My lesson as a homeowner? A window ledge pointed in toward the house is self-destructive. The same is true for each of us: If our foundation is pointed inward toward ourselves, it's self-destructive.

Fulfillment in life comes from making a difference in other people's lives. Our current epidemic of depression and despair comes from an unquenched thirst to serve others. We have become complacent with simply surviving in this noisy, busy world, and survival most often focuses on self or, at best, the people closest to us. Rarely does somebody who's just getting by think of strangers. The danger for most of us comes when we stop believing we can make a difference in others' lives.

Consider the thought process of a young pregnant girl, alone and scared. She may panic to the point of thinking, "I can't even take care of myself; how am I going to take care of a child?"

Without passion and purpose in our lives, we lose sight of our unlimited potential to influence other lives. We may believe only a favored few have the ability to make a difference because they have the power, money, and fame to do something great. This simply isn't true. We each have a unique ability to make a difference, and we must use it to do so. Individualism makes us lose sight of our purpose and our mission. It doesn't bring us happiness; it brings us misery.

MINIMALISM

Derived from the deadly sin of sloth, minimalism is evident in people always asking themselves, "What is the least I can do?" Minimalism has greatly influenced the health care, economic, and vocations crises. Our culture promotes minimalism as another path to happiness. Again, the proof lies in what the culture tries to sell us. If the commercial isn't hedonistic or individualistic, it is most likely minimalistic. A great example is all those pills we love. After all, it doesn't get much easier than taking a pill. See the link between hedonism and minimalism? We don't want somebody on television to tell us we need self-discipline. Instead, we want to hear that we can eat and do whatever we want—as long as we take this magic pill. Please note, I am a doctor who prescribes medication almost daily, and it is a wonderful remedy for those who really need it. However, there are risks to every medication. That is why the last half of the commercial contains the auctioneer voice scaring you to death with all the side effects and telling you to call your doctor right away if you suddenly go blind, get confused, feel depressed, etc. When it comes to our health and physical well-being, we can't keep asking, "What is the least I can do?" We can't keep asking this question in any aspect of life, whether it's school, our job, family, or church.

In college, I had a routine for studying for a final exam. The first half hour of the routine usually consisted of me punching numbers into a calculator. I wasn't trying to solve complicated math problems; I was figuring out how many correct answers I needed for a certain grade! I wanted to know exactly what score I needed on the exam to pass the class. I had all the percentages and scenarios worked out. This, of course, was a total waste of time, and proof I was just jumping through hoops. It was a quest for grades, trying to move on to the next hoop to jump through. Not passionate about the material I was "learning," I never really learned anything from that class. This lack of passion leads to a life of minimalism.

Doing things halfheartedly creates very bad habits. I have always tried to emphasize to my students and athletes that if you aren't putting your heart and soul into what you're doing, then you shouldn't be doing it. Going through the motions only creates bad habits that trickle down into other aspects of our lives. We get into survival mode and begin looking for all the paths of least resistance. This is the link between minimalism and individualism. People in survival mode rarely think of others because they're just trying to survive. It is extremely difficult to think of others' needs when our own needs are not being met.

Being in survival mode robs life of passion and purpose. When we focus on doing and having, we lose sight of who we're becoming. Society tells us if we want to be happy, we must have all the nice things and do all the fun stuff. To be able to do and have these things, we need to make a lot of money. To make a lot of money, we have to go through school and get good grades—at least good enough to pass and get a degree. I suppose that's why I worked so hard to jump through these hoops. It is ironic I always worked hard, which appears to be the opposite of minimalism, but I was working hard at surviving, not thriving.

As long as I was focusing on hoops, I was only concerned about getting through them. This is where minimalism is born. The infamous "What's the least I can do?" question can quickly begin to dominate in life. "What is the least I can do to get through this class in school . . . to keep my wife and children from nagging me . . . to keep my job . . . to still get to heaven?" The list of questions goes on until we're caught in a vicious cycle of survival.

Life then becomes a series of reactions instead of actions. Lacking the mission of "becoming," we focus our attention on the destination and forget about the journey. For example, how many people think that a winning lottery ticket will make them the happiest person in the world? For many people, success in life is finding the quickest and easiest way to have and do the things they want.

In a free country such as the United States of America, the system only works when everyone is doing their best to contribute. In my line of work, I have seen how the system can break down when minimalism and individualism become involved. There are many people who will refuse a higher-paying job because they will lose their Medicaid benefits, which are so much better than the new insurance, for which they would have to "pay." I also have some very bitter patients on Medicaid. I remember one woman in particular, whose glasses broke. She was extremely upset. I watched her cuss out the social worker, who then broke into tears. The woman thought it was a ridiculous service we provided and the frames were worthless. Our company replaces any broken or lost pair of glasses for free, but she didn't care. She felt she was being mistreated, even though she never paid a dime for any glasses. She wanted a high-end frame and was upset that her free "insurance" didn't provide them. She felt her suffering and infirmity earned her the right to have whatever she wanted, and she had lost sight of the fact she lives in a nation that tries to provide for people's needs when they can't afford them.

Government-aided programs to help the poor are wonderful services to humanity; however, they only work under the assumption that all people will try their best to eventually become self-sufficient and even repay their debt to society with their unique talents.

When government aid becomes a crutch that encourages and rewards minimalism, it's no longer a service to society but a burden. There is a fine line between helping people and crippling them. We are all interconnected, and doing things halfheartedly, whether it's at work, home, or church, directly (and indirectly) hurts people around us. We were put here on this earth at this time for a reason—to fulfill a God-given mission. Our destination of sainthood is the same, but our individual journeys are different. We all have a genius, something we were created for to assist in the salvation of mankind. It doesn't matter how big or small we perceive our part to be. If we don't each play that part, it won't get played.

Only thirty-two years old, I don't have as much wisdom and experience in life as many others, but I know that the things in my life that have brought me the most joy and happiness (such as winning a state championship, graduating as an eye doctor, fixing up an old house and making it into a home, running marathons, and mostly, building a family) are the very same things that have brought the most heartache, frustration, suffering, and sacrifice. True love in a fallen world involves suffering. Simply looking at a crucifix should reveal this to us.

47

Life is hard, and God makes this clear to us. In the story of Abraham and Isaac, God says to Abraham, "Take your son Isaac, your only one, whom you love, and go to the land of Moriah. There you shall offer him up as a holocaust on a height that I will point out to you." (Genesis 22:2) He didn't say, "Go to Moriah and I'll tell you what you have to do when you get there." He told him right from the start, "This is going to be hard . . . now walk." He says the same thing to us. Being Christian is hard . . . now walk. Chastity is hard . . . now walk. Being American and living in a free country is hard . . . now walk. Becoming a saint is hard . . . now walk. This story reminds us not only that life is hard, but that everything sacred that we have belongs to the Father. Our spouse, children, job, money, home, possessions, talent, and our very lives all belong to God. Like Abraham, we must be willing to take everything we have to Moriah and offer them back to God if we are to discover their purpose. Sometimes we have to be willing to give up our way to discover God's way. A free country is not a country where everyone has a right to have and do whatever they want and everyone deserves to "get rich quick." A free country is a place where everyone has the opportunity to reach his or her fullest potential. You will never reach that potential without making sacrifices. Sacrifices don't help God, but they help us. The path of least resistance will not bring us happiness. Minimalism prevents us from becoming the saint we were created to be.

THE ROOT OF THE PROBLEM

These are just a few examples of hedonism, minimalism, and individualism. Hopefully you'll be able to start recognizing them in your everyday life. They are powerful and destructive diseases and are certainly not new. So where did they come from? They have evolved from generation to generation, and we can find examples in every culture throughout the history of humanity.

In optometry school, a common saying I heard when learning how to cure ocular disease was, "To kill the fruit, you have to get to the root." If we're really serious about curing this outbreak of these horrible diseases in our own culture, then we must stop treating their symptoms and get to the root of the problem, back to their origin. We have to go back to the beginning, and look to the book of Genesis.

Genesis, particularly Chapter 3 (the story of the fall of mankind), gives us answers to so many of our modern-day problems, and teaches each of us something about ourselves. I have discovered so much from this story, and each time I hear it, I learn something new about myself.

Read this story with a new set of eyes, and listen carefully for the birth of hedonism, individualism, and minimalism. This story is the game film of the opponent, so we can learn much about our enemy and how he works.

THE GAME FILM

Now the serpent was the most cunning of all the animals the Lord God had made. The serpent asked the woman, "Did God really tell you not to eat from any of the trees in the garden?" The woman answered the serpent: "We may eat of the fruit of the trees in the garden; it is only about the fruit of the tree in the middle of the garden that God said, 'You shall not eat it or even touch it, lest you die.'" But the serpent said to the woman: "You certainly will not die! No, God knows well that the moment

49

you eat of it your eyes will be opened and you will be like gods who know what is good and what is bad." The woman saw that the tree was good for food, pleasing to the eyes, and desirable for gaining wisdom. So she took some of its fruit and ate it; and she also gave some to her husband, who was with her, and he ate it. Then the eyes of both of them were opened, and they realized that they were naked; so they sewed fig leaves together and made loincloths for themselves. (Genesis 3:1–7)

I mentioned this is the game film of the enemy. To really learn from this story, we need to read it in slow motion. We need to break it down step by step to see Satan's strategy. Satan is represented by the serpent, and when he approaches the woman, what's the first thing he tries to do? He tries to make God look unreasonable. He says to the woman, "Did God really say you couldn't eat any of this fruit?" How often do we hear this question in the context of the Church? Does the Catholic Church *really* say you can't use contraception? Does the Church *really* say you have to go to Mass every Sunday? Does the Church *really* tell you not to live together before marriage? By attempting to make God look unreasonable, Satan provokes a specific question from the woman. He is advocating individualism by prompting her to ask, "What's in it for me?" His attempt initially fails, and she counters him by saying, "That's not what God said. God said we could eat any of the fruit, just not the fruit from that tree there in the middle. We can't eat it or even touch it or we'll die."

Having failed at making God look unreasonable, Satan then goes on to call God a liar. "You will not die," he says. "If you eat that fruit you will become like God, knowing good from evil." Here is where minimalism is born. Satan is saying if we want to be happy, all we have to do is eat the forbidden fruit. It is that simple. And of course, the forbidden fruit is to attempt to choose for yourself what is right and what is wrong. God created us with free will so we could choose to *do* good or to *do* evil, but we'll never have the power to choose what *is* good and what *is* evil. Satan entices us to deny objective truth. If we can be like God and decide what is good and evil, then we don't need his rules and regulations holding us back. We begin to rationalize, "What is wrong for you isn't necessarily wrong for me because I get to choose what is right and wrong for me." Satan successfully convinces the woman that God doesn't love her, implying God does not want her to be like him; that God is holding something back, and if she wants to be happy she's going to have to reach out and grasp it for herself because God isn't going to give it to her.

So now, after capturing the woman's attention with individualism and minimalism, Satan seals the deal with hedonism. We read, "The woman saw that the tree was good for food, pleasing to the eyes, and desirable for gaining wisdom." So she sees the fruit, desires and eats it. Eve gives it to her husband, who eats the fruit; then, the eyes of both are opened, and they realize they are naked.

Later in Genesis Chapter 3, God comes and questions the couple—and then the blame game starts. God asks Eve why she ate the fruit, and she blames the serpent. Remember, the story isn't about Adam and Eve; it's about you and me. We also blame the serpent. We use the excuse, "The devil made me do it." We say, "We couldn't help it; it's not our fault. We were deceived." It is imperative to remember where the war takes place—inside the human heart. I keep repeating this sentence so you will remember. No force on earth, and none in hell, can take your will from you. Your will is yours. You choose.

God also asks Adam why he ate the fruit. Adam's response is interesting. Most people would say Adam blames the woman, but this isn't true. Look at the response carefully. Genesis 3:12 states: "The man replied, 'The woman whom you put here with me, she gave me the fruit from the tree, and so I ate it.'" Adam doesn't blame the woman; he blames God because God gave him the woman. Adam represents every man. We all blame God from time to time. When we're lustful, greedy, or gluttonous, we blame God for giving us these temptations. We say to God, "You gave me these temptations. You gave me these hormones. You gave me these desires. You gave me this lack of ability. You gave me this lot in life. You gave me this hopeless situation. It is your fault."

As their creator, God warned Adam and Eve not to fall for the lies of the serpent, but they used their free will to disobey him. When speaking to engaged couples, I always use the following analogy: Imagine God gives you a new house as a wedding present. He says it's your house and you can do whatever you want with it. Paint the walls whatever color you like, and remodel the rooms as you want—but you can't take out the center beam. You think to yourself, "This is my house now; I should be allowed to do whatever I want, so I am taking out that center beam."

The moment you take out the center beam, the whole house comes crashing down. What do you do? You blame God, of course, because he is the one who gave you the house, and he didn't prevent the house from falling down. You ignore the fact that God told you not to remove the center beam. God doesn't prevent the consequences of our actions from happening. He allows nature to take its course. Like Adam and Eve, we often take the attitude of, "It's not my fault." We fall for Satan's lies and see God as an unjust dictator who doesn't really love us.

TRUE LOVE HURTS

We were created to serve, and serving is hard. That is why we prefer blissful ignorance as opposed to knowing our mission. The world tells us to avoid suffering at all costs because the world teaches, "If it feels good, do it," and not "If it involves suffering, do it." However, the reality is, because of the story you just read from Genesis Chapter 3, to live is to suffer. This is the wisdom of John Paul II. In his apostolic letter *Salvifici Deloris,* on the salvific meaning of human suffering, John Paul II writes, "It can be said that man in a special fashion becomes the way for the Church when suffering enters his life. This happens, as we know, at different moments in life, it takes place in different ways, it assumes different dimensions; nevertheless, in whatever form, suffering seems to be, and is, almost *inseparable from man's earthly existence."*

You can't avoid suffering in a fallen world, because it is part of our fallen nature. So, continue a little further into Genesis Chapter 3 to see the consequences of original sin. God says to the woman, "I will intensify the pangs of your childbearing; in pain shall you bring forth children. Yet your urge shall be for your husband, and he shall be your master." To the man he says, "Cursed be the ground because of you! In toil shall you eat its yield all the days of your life . . . by the sweat of your face shall you get bread to eat . . ." (Genesis 3:16–19)

What is God describing here? He is describing the family unit. All of a sudden, to love as God loves is hard and involves suffering. It is precisely this link between true love and suffering that the culture rejects, which is why the family unit is under attack. God isn't imposing his wrath on us with this declaration that suffering will now be a part of life; he is giving us the love of a good father. He is showing mercy. God is coming down to us and telling us that we don't understand what it means to love as he loves. He doesn't just tell us how to love. Every time we see a crucifix we should be reminded that true love involves suffering. God teaches us this lesson in life by allowing us to experience fruitful suffering. Experience is the best teacher. I learned this lesson the hard way.

A TOUGH LESSON

A few months before my graduation from optometry school, my wife and I found out we were expecting our second child. We were excited. We'd had a lot of difficulty conceiving our first child, which had left us with the fear of infertility, but this child had come with very little stress. The only problem was we were a bit naive about how the world worked. I had been a student my whole life. I'd had student health insurance. My wife had stopped teaching when our first child was born, so we'd lost her insurance. I had planned on purchasing health insurance after graduation. Shopping around, I was quickly informed that no health insurance company in its right mind would pick up a pregnant woman. I was losing my student insurance, and no insurance company would cover us until the baby was born.

I remember thinking they couldn't possibly be allowed to do this. But I was wrong. I wasn't an employee, and didn't even have a job yet. My plan had been to move back to my previous college town and work with my mentoring doctor. He was going to allow me to use his building to establish my own patient base. The problem was no health insurance was involved. I suddenly realized the gravity of my lack of planning and knowledge of "real life." Here we were, expecting our second child, and I had no job. The contract with the doctor I was joining started falling through after the lawyers began reviewing it. My plan to buy into the practice was ruined. We had already bought a house that was in extremely poor condition. We had no health insurance. Our first pregnancy had ended in a Cesarean section delivery, which we were told was about a twelve-thousand-dollar surgery. That put us at a much greater risk for having another C-section. I didn't have twelve thousand dollars. We were scared, more afraid than you can imagine.

One day that summer our parish priest came over for supper to bless our house and get to know us. I was particularly stressed that day, with one side of the roof shingles torn off but not covered with tar paper. The tarp over the roof wasn't working very well, and rain from the previous day was dripping into what would eventually be the master bedroom. Buckets were set out catching the water. The living room was the only finished room in the house. Our mattress was on the floor, and all of our dishes were on bookshelves. My pregnant wife was doing all the cooking sitting on the floor because we had no cabinets or countertops.

I had just blown a fuse in the house, which had caused me to blow a fuse myself. At the fuse box cursing up a storm, I didn't realize the parish priest had already arrived and was standing by the door. Talk about a bad first impression. He was a wonderful priest, though, and his cool, calm demeanor made me instantly feel better. I told him my worries and fears that day, how I was in over my head. He told me to trust God, and that everything was going to be okay. I asked him to pray for me and to pray that it didn't rain until I fixed my roof. Wouldn't you know, it didn't rain for the next three weeks!

Knowing the only way to get health insurance would be to get a job as an employee of a company that provided this benefit, I applied at a package handling company because it offered health insurance for part-time work. At first my application was ignored, so I applied again. Finally, four months before the baby was due, I was hired to unload packages from semi trucks as fast as I could from three to nine a.m.

The work was demanding, and the turnover rate was really high. In five months, they went through several employees. One coworker, a large college football player, worked for half a day, left at break time, and never came back. Sometimes I worked inside a semi truck with a man named Tiny, and as you can imagine, he was anything but tiny. He also had a bit of a temper, and I was honestly afraid of being inside that semi with him. Most people who worked there had at least one or two other jobs. Tiny was a bartender and a bouncer. I am pretty sure I was the only one there whose second job was as an eye doctor.

In addition to working at the package handling company, I worked in two offices seeing patients. Many days, my schedule was to get up at two a.m., drive to work, unload semis from three to nine, shower at the university, go straight to one of my offices and work until one p.m., then drive an hour to the other office and work until five, then drive an hour back home. Needless to say, I was tired, and I didn't always handle my situation very well. I was irritable and grouchy. One month before the baby was born, the health insurance took effect, and everything was paid for from the very start of the pregnancy to the end. I am truly grateful to that package handling company. Originally I was bitter about getting paid eight dollars an hour after eight years of college education, but the opportunity to provide health care for my family was worth a lot more than my paycheck.

When the baby was finally born, I felt as though I had earned this child. I assumed that God was going to reward me with a well-mannered and easygoing baby. I assumed wrong. Hannah, our second daughter, developed quite a bad case of colic that lasted for many months. My wife and I walked with our screaming baby girl for hours and hours each night, taking turns for as long as we could handle it before we needed to switch. I honestly don't know how single parents do it. A baby is a two-person job.

One night, as Hannah was screaming, I took my frustrations to God, telling him it wasn't fair. I was trying to do what I thought he wanted me to do, trying to be open to life. What had I done to deserve this? Why couldn't I get my baby girl to stop crying? I had given her everything I could think would help, laying down my life so she could be born. Yet she wouldn't stop crying.

As usual, God's gentle reply came to me in the depths of my heart. I suddenly realized that my whole life I'd been asking God for things I thought would make me happy. My whole life, God has been granting my requests. As a child, I dreamed of playing hockey. I had never even seen a real ice rink, and all I wanted was to one day play in a real game on a real sheet of ice. I prayed for that opportunity. I went on to play in multiple recreation leagues in high school and then four years of college hockey, traveling around the country to play. On two occasions, I scored the game-winning goal in overtime. Yet I still complained. It wasn't enough for me—I wanted to play on the NCAA team, and I wanted to be more successful.

In junior high, I saw my older brothers run in the state track meet. I prayed that one day I would be good enough to run at state, and even stand on the podium. I went on to stand on every step of the podium, placing first, second, third, fourth, fifth, sixth, and seventh in the state throughout my career. Yet when I left the stadium for the last time, my prayer to God was, "How could you let me fail in this way?"

I prayed for a good career and went on to become an eye doctor with the opportunity to do something I love and make a difference in people's lives. Every day I get to look into the human eye, which is one of the most divine designs in the universe. Yet I still complain about the petty details of my work.

I prayed for a wife and children, and here I was, with a wife more perfect for me than I could have ever imagined and two beautiful baby girls, yet I stood there asking God, "What have I done to deserve this punishment?" My whole life God has given me everything I've asked for tenfold. He laid down his life so I could live. Everything I need to be happy has been given to me as a free gift. Yet I hadn't stopped crying. In very plain English, I heard God saying, "Welcome to my world. You say you have laid down your life so your child could live? Think of all you have suffered and sacrificed for your child, multiply it by infinity, take it to the depths of eternity, and you'll still barely have a glimpse of how much I suffered for you. Now, despite all you have been through, think of how much you still love your child and how much more you would be willing to go through for her. Take that love, multiply it by infinity, take it to the depths of eternity, and you'll still barely have a glimpse of how much I love you." Sometimes, a parent needs to let his or her children suffer so they can learn a great lesson. God is the perfect father. His love is not puppy love, it is parent love. There will be suffering, but there will be fruit from that suffering.

However, the enemy tries to prevent us from learning this lesson, telling us that God is trying to keep us from being happy. The enemy tries to use God's own weapon against him by making the claim that to prevent suffering is an act of mercy. This is why we have "mercy killing" and why we terminate pregnancies. We must not fall for the lies of the enemy and must always remember that God is a loving father who desires mercy, not sacrifice, but he uses sacrifice to create mercy.

THE PERFECT LIE

As I mentioned earlier, Satan is a genius and his strategy works to perfection. We are tempted to say Adam and Eve were just plain stupid to fall for the deception, and that we would never do what they did. However, the story isn't about Adam and Eve; it's about mankind, our ancestors of ages past, and our own generation. It is about you and me. Let's pinpoint the steps in Satan's strategy and see how they apply to our present culture.

> Step 1: Satan removes God from the picture. God is love, and God is truth.
>
> Step 2: Satan introduces the lie, the counterfeit, to replace the truth.
>
> Step 3: Satan enslaves us when we take the bait.

Now let's take a look at the culture and the country in which we live. The United States was founded on Christian principles, and on our currency are the words "In God we Trust." However, over time we began to argue over religion. Perhaps some over-zealous people tried to force their religion on others. People saw the fighting and the arguing, and they associated the turmoil with religion. Because of this, some very well-meaning people suggested we should keep our religion to ourselves. The thought was that religion can be practiced in the privacy of your own home or church, but let's keep religion out of the public eye because it's offensive to people.

MORAL RELATIVISM

We wanted to guarantee freedom of religion, but we accomplished the exact opposite. Whether we realize it or not, we've fallen for the lie that if we want to be happy and have peace, all we have to do is eat from the tree of knowledge of good and evil. All we have to do is remove objective truth, and we can choose our own truth. This leads us down a slippery slope. Nobody wants to be offensive, and we think there will be no more fighting if we just keep our beliefs to ourselves. What's wrong for me doesn't necessarily have to be wrong for you.

A survey done by the Marist Institute for Public Opinion in January 2010 found that eighty-two percent of Catholic "millennials" (those age eighteen to twenty-nine) agreed with the statement that "morals are relative; that is, there is no definite right or wrong for everybody."[7] Now people can use the infamous excuse, "Well I believe this is wrong, but I don't want to push my morals on someone else."

Abortion is a perfect example of this excuse. My wife and I once had an in-depth discussion on this subject with some very close friends of ours. These friends are people we greatly admire and respect, and we were surprised to learn their views differed from ours on this subject. Too often we have a narrow-minded view of our beliefs. We perceive that we're good, and anybody who doesn't believe what we believe is bad. This conversation with these wonderful people helped us learn others generally want to do good; we all have good intentions.

Even though our views on abortion were different, our intentions were the same—both wanting to do what was right, wanting to help people. Controversial subjects such as abortion are not about good people versus bad people. Looking back at this discussion, I don't think I handled it very well. The other couple's view was that abortion is a way of preventing suffering. Their point on morality was that not everybody believes that life begins at conception. Again, they were implying that it's okay for me to believe life begins at conception, but it's not okay to force my beliefs on others who don't believe the same thing.

I spent a lot of energy trying to get them to believe what I believe, which is a frustrating and often a losing cause. Evangelizing isn't about telling people what to do and what to believe. People are on different parts of their journeys, and forcing our beliefs isn't the way to show them the truth. However, we must live our beliefs; otherwise, we're hypocrites. We must be careful not to fall for moral relativism, which is basically the destruction of objective truth.

As C. S. Lewis once said, "Christianity, if false, is of no importance; and if true, of infinite importance. The one thing it cannot be is moderately important." The same can be said on the issue of abortion. I believe with all my heart that life begins at conception, that at the moment of conception, something has changed forever. It is not only a human being purposely created by a loving God; it's an eternal soul who will never cease to exist. This is either true or it isn't. If it's true, then the only reaction to abortion is to fight for the lives of the unborn. In the case of the unborn, it's not a fight against prejudice or persecution. It is a fight against annihilation. We are fighting for the right to live. To fight does not mean we create violence, but it does mean that we must live and speak the truth, even if it offends people.

If the U.S. government created a law legalizing murder of the elderly or the handicapped because they redefined the definition of a human being, how would moral relativists react? Would they say these actions are okay as long as you believe what you're doing is right? Would they say, "I believe the elderly and handicapped are human beings, but if other people don't, I can't force them to accept my morals." Hitler thought he was doing something noble to improve humanity. He didn't sit around thinking about what kind of evil he could do. Does that make his actions any less appalling? It doesn't matter what he believes; there's an objective truth, and murdering people is always wrong.

This battle can't be won by force. We can't win by changing people's minds; we can only win by changing hearts. We must begin to live our beliefs. We must offer an example of truth if we expect others to find it. If we expect others to see children as a gift and expect them to suffer for the greater good, we must be willing to suffer as well. We must be willing to lay down our lives for our children. Raising children is always hard and always involves dying to self, or giving up your own desires for the good of another. No matter who you are or what your situation, a million dollars can't buy a child's temperament. Believe me, I've tried to pay my children to stop throwing temper tantrums. It doesn't work!

Money can buy babysitters, designer clothes, and expensive video games, but it is often more of an obstacle to being a good parent than a necessity. When all you have to give is yourself and your love, then your child is more likely to get you and your love, which is what he or she truly needs. The wonderful irony is that giving yourself and your love is what you truly need as well. If abortion is justifiable in cases in which suffering and hardship will come from the birth of the child, then every pregnancy should be terminated, because suffering in life can't be avoided. A culture that destroys children is a culture with no hope. It is a culture that has found no meaning in suffering. Becoming who you were born to be is not only the greatest thing you can do for yourself; it's also the greatest thing you can do for humanity, and the best evangelizing tool.

RUFFLING FEATHERS

Our Christian faith is an important part of who we are, but now we're being asked to leave that part of ourselves at home and at church. Remember, we're discussing Satan's first step, to remove God from the picture. When we go to work or school, we're supposed to leave our religion at the door. We are asked to live divided lives, to be one person on Sunday and a different person the rest of the week. In public, it's common courtesy not to mention religion. No religious symbols can be present in public institutions or public areas because we don't want to offend anyone. This is not freedom of religion; this is destruction of religion.

Scripture tells us that God is a jealous God, and he should come first in everything we do (see Exodus 20:5). We can't push him off to the side when he is inconvenient to us. We are not teachers who are Christian; we're Christian teachers. We are not doctors who are Christian; we're Christian doctors. We are not engineers who are Christian; we're Christian engineers. We are not custodians who are Christian; we're Christian custodians. If we call ourselves Christian, God comes first, no matter who we are or what we're doing.

Removing God from the public circle is not healthy for any culture. George Washington said in his farewell address, "Whatever may be conceded to the influence of refined education on minds of peculiar structure, reason and experience both forbid us to expect, that national morality can prevail in exclusion of religious principle."[8] God represents what is good and true whether you believe in him or not. "Thou shall not lie" is one of the Ten Commandments. Should we ban schools from teaching children

63

that lying is bad because it promotes religion?

Removing God from the culture leaves disorder, destruction, and chaos. It is wrong and offensive to speak maliciously of and attack other people. It is also wrong to try to force beliefs and opinions on others. However, I don't see it as offensive to practice our own beliefs. How is prayer in school violating religious rights? I attended a friend's college graduation at a state university several years back, and at the graduation ceremony a prayer was recited. The man seated beside me made a comment that perhaps this was inappropriate since the university is not religiously affiliated. His point was that there are people from other countries and religious backgrounds attending the university, and the prayer may have made them feel uncomfortable. Why? I don't remember any part of the prayer condemning or disrespecting anybody. When did acknowledging God become offensive? We live in a culture where it is legal to hand kids condoms in school but not bibles.

People argue that some religions offend others, and by practicing our own religion we may offend somebody else's. A recent news article discussed a professor at the University of Illinois who was fired for teaching the Catholic stance on homosexuality to his class. The class was called Introduction to Catholicism. He was fired for making the comment that "homosexual acts violate natural moral law." A student complained, stating, "Teaching a student about the tenets of a religion is one thing. Declaring that homosexual acts violate the natural laws of man is another. The courses at this institution should be geared to contribute to the public discourse and promote independent thought; not limit one's worldview and ostracize people of a certain sexual orientation."[9]

The teacher was fired because he taught a Catholic principle in a class introducing people to Catholicism. What he said was a tenet of a religion. Our culture is attempting to avoid offending anybody, which simply isn't possible. The man didn't say homosexuals are evil people. In fact, he made a point to tell the students he was talking about homosexual acts, not tendencies. We all have disordered tendencies and desires.

The Church simply teaches that acting on disordered tendencies and giving in to temptation is immoral and self-destructive. The Church says the same thing about pornography, infidelity, and fornication. Homosexuality is a topic that is so focused on acceptance and tolerance that morality is pushed aside. We should always accept people and never harass or judge anyone. Every human being deserves to be treated with love and respect, but that is precisely the point. Just because you desire something doesn't mean it's good and it doesn't mean you are doomed to act on that desire. You aren't loving and respecting somebody by encouraging him or her to do something that is self-destructive. The professor who was fired did not judge or discriminate against anybody. He simply stated a fact regarding Catholic teaching—the whole point of the class. There are many things about the Catholic faith that some people disagree with and find offensive. If he were to try to explain why Catholicism teaches that sexual promiscuity, premarital sex, and contraception are immoral, somebody could have complained about him ostracizing people with certain sexual preferences. Students have every right to express their beliefs and opinions in a respectful way. This is healthy dialogue. But so does the professor, who did not force his beliefs on them. Thankfully, enough people had the courage to stand up and defend this man, and he was awarded his job back.

In my first year of college, I was required to attend a diversity seminar class. I attended a Christian-affiliated university, yet in this diversity class, the professor taught her opinion that homosexuality is a normal and natural lifestyle. She also spent class time teaching how masturbation is natural and normal. This, in my opinion, is much more offensive to teach at a Christian-affiliated university than is teaching the tenets of the Catholic faith in a Catholic class at a public university. I regret that I didn't possess the courage at the time to respectfully speak up and disagree with her.

I try to give blood to the American Red Cross as often as possible. One of the questions you have to answer before giving blood is, "If you are a male, have you had sexual contact with another male, even once, since 1977?" Some government leaders are now trying to remove this question because it's offensive to those with same-sex attraction. The fact is, the homosexual lifestyle is dangerous, especially pertaining to HIV. The risk of contracting HIV and other STDs is greatly increased for homosexual males. Two people of the same sex may have feelings for each other, but love is much more than a feeling. Homosexual action puts both people in grave danger. The act is no more an act of love than me allowing my children to eat junk food for breakfast, lunch, and dinner. They may desire junk food for three meals each day, but giving it to them would be harmful to their health. It would give them pleasure, but not happiness. I love my children with all my heart, but love doesn't mean giving them everything they want. Love is choosing what's best for your beloved.

The U.S. Food and Drug Administration website gives multiple reasons why male homosexual acts make someone ineligible to donate blood. The first one: "Men who have had sex with men since 1977 have an HIV prevalence (the total number of cases of a disease that are present in a population at a specific point in time) 60 times higher than the general population, 800 times higher than first time blood donors and 8,000 times higher than repeat blood donors (American Red Cross). Even taking into account that 75% of HIV infected men who have sex with men already know they are HIV positive and would be unlikely to donate blood, the HIV prevalence in potential donors with history of male sex with males is 200 times higher than first time blood donors and 2,000 times higher than repeat blood donors." [10] This is from the FDA, the government agency we trust to keep us safe.

Medical professionals have been largely silent on this issue, which I don't understand. There are varying studies on the health risks of the homosexual lifestyle, but every study I have seen clearly points to the fact that this lifestyle is dangerous. Statistics from studies need to be taken with a grain of salt, and I'm well aware that you can find a study to tell you almost anything you want to hear. However, I've tried to find studies showing homosexual acts are safe. I can't find any. One study found that out of 6,574 homosexual deaths, the average life span, if AIDS was the cause of death, was 39. The average life span if AIDS was not the cause, 42. For lesbians, the average life span was 44. [11] Yet we don't want to offend people, so we're willing to put them and others in danger? The medical community seems to have no problem telling people that smoking is unhealthy, even though many people get offended and don't want to hear it. Why can't medical professionals also be honest about homosexuality, which has been shown to be even more deadly than smoking? We must choose to do what is best for the people we love, and encourage them to do what is best for themselves.

FALLING FOR DECEPTIONS

Another example of destruction of religion is the issue with pharmacies, hospitals, charities, insurance companies, schools, and religious organizations. On January 20, 2012, the U.S. Department of Health and Human Services declared that every employer must provide contraception and abortion-inducing drugs in their insurance plans. Government officials are also trying to make it a requirement for pharmacists to fill prescriptions for the contraceptive pill and emergency contraception. The idea is to make sure every woman in America has access to contraception, sterilization, and abortion-inducing drugs because they feel these things are "essential" to a woman's health as preventative medicine. Abortion and contraception are directly opposed to Catholic teaching. This contraceptive mentality in health care makes the assumption that pregnancy is a disease! Children are not the disease (they are often the cure, teaching us to take the focus off of self).Unwanted pregnancies are not the problem, they are the symptom. The problems are hedonism, individualism, and minimalism. People are making poor choices, and when pregnancy occurs they see themselves as victims, and do not want to take responsibility for their actions. Instead of encouraging people to make better choices, the government promotes contraception and abortion as a solution to the problems that arise from poor choices. They call it freedom of choice, but it's actually the opposite. It is an attitude of defeat that assumes people are not free to choose. It assumes people simply can't choose to do what is right.

Sexual relations outside the context of marriage and at younger ages more likely results in unwanted pregnancies, STDs, depression, and broken relationships. Yet we actually hand condoms to young people and promote birth control pills as a form of responsibility. What message are we sending? Demanding contraception for everyone is no different than saying to your ten-year-old son, "I would rather you didn't ride your bike down the middle of the interstate, but I know you are going to do it anyway. So here, wear this helmet. That way, when you get hit by the oncoming semi, you might not die. You will just be crippled for the rest of your life."

The Catholic Church has always taught that sex is something sacred, reserved for husband and wife within the context of a loving marriage open to new life. It is a renewal of wedding vows. Marital love meets the sacrifices and demands of laying down your life for your spouse and children freely, totally, faithfully, and fruitfully. The marital love between a man and a woman is a great power and a great responsibility. In cases in which a married couple is not ready for another child, natural family planning (NFP) is a great way to space children. It is proven to be ninety-eight to ninety-nine percent effective, it has no bad side effects, and it works with God's design in the natural rhythm of life. However, very few doctors and government officials are promoting this proven way to space children because it involves a little bit of self-discipline and requires communication between partners and periodic abstinence. NFP requires a committed relationship and focuses on love, whereas as condoms, birth control pills, and sterilization focus on "protection" from the harms of lust.

Many people understand why the Church would be offended at the idea of providing abortion to employees, but not contraception. Catholics combating this HHS mandate are quick to point out the issue is about religious freedom and not contraception. First and foremost, it is about religious freedom, but it is also about contraception, because if contraception really is "essential health care", then the Church rightfully should have to provide it. The whole point is that contraception is NOT essential health care, or even health care at all. What disease is it preventing? It does not make our bodies healthier, and is in fact a threat to health. Read all the side effects and health risks on the package insert of the pill, which include things such as stroke, heart attack, gallbladder disease, liver tumors, cancer, and blood clots. The culture believes the "benefit" of sterilization outweighs these risks.

We must stop speaking as if we are embarrassed about the Church teaching on contraception. The Church is not an old demented woman that we have to respect just because of her age. We must respect her because she is right. She is guided by the Holy Spirit, and her wisdom far exceeds ours. We should take comfort in the words Jesus said about his Church, "The gates of the netherworld shall not prevail against it." (Matthew 16:18)

If we look closely, we will see that contraception and abortion are fruits of the same tree, and both have always been considered intrinsically wrong by the Catholic Church as well as all protestant churches up until 1930. It is not a new issue, and you can find quotes condemning contraception from early church fathers, early church councils, and all the protestant reformers, including Martin Luther, John Calvin, and John Wesley.[12]

The contraceptive pill has several modes of action, one of which can actually work like abortion. High levels of estrogen are not safe, so the modern-day pill uses much lower dosages of estrogen, which leaves a much higher potential for breakthrough ovulation. However, the pill also thins the lining of the uterus, which can prevent a fertilized egg from implanting. This possible mechanism of action is still considered contraception by medical professionals because they simply define pregnancy as implantation, not fertilization (conception). For those who believe life begins at conception, this is problematic. It is an abortive mechanism of action, yet most women, even many Catholic women, quite happily use the pill, ignorant of how it can really work.

By requiring Catholic institutions to pay for contraceptives and abortifacient drugs, the government is forcing them to violate their own consciences. Not only are we not allowed to live our beliefs; we're being required to act against them. The Church's mission is to help people and respect the dignity of every human life, and providing contraception and abortion as "essential health care" to other people destroys life and encourages destructive behavior. Again, it's not freedom of religion; it's the destruction of it.

Contrary to public opinion, the Church does not force her teachings on anybody, and nobody should force the Church to go against her teachings. People get angry at the Church not because she is forcing them to act a certain way, but because she refuses to condone their actions. People want the Church's approval so they don't feel guilty. The truth is, so many people disagree with the Church on issues of sexuality not because her teachings are wrong, but because they are hard. When it comes to health care, there is no doubt the Church's stance of abstinence before marriage and fidelity to the wedding vows in marriage promotes stronger families and healthier bodies. People are angry because the Church challenges them to be free, and we want to convince ourselves we are victims to our passions and desires. We like our captivity. We have the freedom to choose not to follow the Church's teachings, but nobody should be able to force the Church to go against her teachings.

I understand that issues regarding sexual morality, such as homosexuality and contraception, are very difficult issues in the modern world. More Catholics ignore Church teaching on these issues probably more than any other issue. However, I hope you will take the time to at least research why the Church teaches what she does. I must say, the Church has not always done a good job explaining why contraception and homosexuality are wrong, and most people just don't know. If they truly knew and understood the beauty of Church's teachings, I don't think most people would act against them. I have pointed out some physical dangers of contraception and homosexuality, but the spiritual aspects are the most convincing if we are willing to open our minds and hearts to the wisdom of the Church.

John Paul II's teaching, The Theology of the Body, is a tremendous tool to help rediscover the beauty of Catholic teaching. In these 129 addresses given between 1979 and 1984, John Paul II helps us understand the meaning of our bodies and the very meaning of life. We come to understand the body is good; it is sacred. Satan attacks what is sacred. He removes the truth of love and replaces it with the counterfeit of lust. The Theology of the Body attempts to point us back to the truth of love. It is not condemning or restricting, it is inviting and liberating. It was one of John Paul II's first teachings as Pope, and one of his greatest weapons against what he called the culture of death. The confusion about the meaning of our bodies and sexuality is perhaps one of the greatest victories for the enemy in the last century.

We can't continue to fall for the lies of the serpent who wants us to see God as an unloving master and not a father. God wants us to be happy more than we want it for ourselves; he loves us more than we love ourselves. We must trust him and his church. We must stop asking, "What's in it for me?" which is step one of Satan's strategy. This question focuses on individual wants instead of universal rights. It takes only one individual to say, "God, and any mention of God, offends me," and we remove God from the culture. By removing God from the culture, we remove objective truth. By removing objective truth, we have no guiding principles. Without guiding principles, we have no meaning and purpose. This is self-destructive. We must stop living divided lives. We must live our faith, even if it may offend some people, and even if it is hard. The reality is, if Catholics don't start living their faith in America, they soon may not have the freedom to live their faith. One of the primary reasons cited for enforcing government regulations that are offensive to the Catholic faith is that most Catholics don't follow what the Church teaches anyway. However, morality is not a democracy decided by popular vote. The Church will always proclaim the truth, even if she stands alone, and even if she offends some people. Jesus offended many people, but he didn't water down truth. He was not interested in helping people cope with or tolerate their sins; he was only interested in setting them free from them.

LIES, LIES, LIES

A Godless culture leaves us as orphans. We have no Father, we have no objective truth to lead us, so now we search for happiness in all the wrong places. Once Satan has removed God from the culture (Step 1 of his strategy), he has every opportunity to introduce the counterfeits. This is Step 2 of his three-step process we saw in Genesis Chapter 3. Satan is the father of lies. He has successfully convinced us that God doesn't love us, and that God is holding something back. His solution is to break free from the rules and regulations God uses to "hold us back" and reach for happiness in the things of this world.

Satan tempts us with material gain and physical pleasure. He entices us to build our lives around doing the things we feel like doing and having the things we want to have. Removing God, we have forgotten that life is about who we become—not what we do and what we have. In Satan's world, it's all about "me," all about feeling good on the path of least resistance. Hedonism, minimalism, and individualism are not only contagious, but addictive.

Satan's third and final step in his plan is to enslave us, and enslave us he has. We lead lives of a thousand addictions. We are always left wanting more, never satisfied. Is your heart a sink with an open drain? We fill our hearts with the lies of the world that seem to satisfy for a short time, but then we are empty again. It becomes a vicious cycle. It is a sure sign of slavery, a common theme throughout salvation history.

The captivity and exile of God's people is noted throughout the Bible. In the book of Exodus, Pharaoh kept the Hebrews in slavery by making them constantly work, so they had no time to serve God. They were so busy doing, they could not become. They became complacent in their captivity and began worshiping Egyptian gods. They accepted the reality of what they were given. When Moses led them to freedom, what happened? They complained and wanted to go back—they were used to their cells.

So many people today, without even realizing it, worship false gods and can't let go of these counterfeits. So busy with the things of this world, they have no time for God. They remain in bondage because they actually like being exiled from God. They are afraid to be freed from their cells, which they prefer. And Satan is strong—alone we are powerless to break free, but the good news is we aren't alone and God wants to help us break free.

There is an antidote to the culture of death and the culture of lies. It is easy to give up, to just say we're doomed, but I believe the cross has power. Jesus Christ did not die for nothing. He proves to us that God is our ally. Through his death and resurrection, there is hope. I refuse to empty the cross of its power. It is time for this sleeping giant, the Church of God, to wake up. A revival is on the horizon.

MISSION 2

Applying the Second Step to Winning the War Within

UNPLUG

Wait! Before you throw this book aside, let me at least explain this second mission. For many Americans, television, the Internet, and the radio are another member of the family. Growing up, it seemed like our TV was always on. Turning on the TV was one of the first things we did after walking in the door (it was actually second—first we raided the fridge). I don't want to convince you televisions, computers, or radios are evil. In fact, I'm a very visual person—being an eye doctor and all—and have a large-screen HDTV hanging on the wall in my basement. I appreciate that technology can almost make it look like I'm at the game. (And my excuse for buying the TV was that I wanted to childproof my basement, and didn't want any sharp corners at eye level. Hence, a TV that hangs on the wall was a "necessity"!)

The TV itself isn't evil. It is the content on the TV that's the problem. Over the years, messages and images displayed over the airwaves have gradually degenerated so that almost every show is now infested with hedonism, individualism, and minimalism. Satan has successfully created his own twenty-four-hour-a-day infomercial.

There is still good programming, but a lot of really entertaining shows seem to promote a good message, only to have some blatant lies thrown into the moral of the story. Once again, we see how Satan is a genius, using a strategy of ninety percent truth to get his ten percent of lies across. [13] I challenge you to unplug your television for one month, and see how the atmosphere in your home changes. Perhaps you could replace television with spiritual reading. I suspect this mission is impossible for many of you at this time. If you're in the habit of watching several hours of TV each day, then it may be really difficult to cut it out cold turkey. If this is true, you know that you have an addiction to overcome. The best way to overcome an addiction may be little by little.

If you need to start by cutting out TV one night a week, so be it, but start this mission in one form or another. We love what is most familiar to us. If you've watched *Wheel of Fortune* every night for the past twenty years, you may have trouble letting go. I'm not suggesting shows like this are bad, but even if you are giving up "good" shows for one month, it won't harm you. It will be a good test to see if you really are free from them. Too much of anything can be bad, unless it's God. Addiction is an increasing desire for something that gives less and less satisfaction. Spending time with and for God cannot be addicting, because if it's truly God, it won't give you less satisfaction, only more. No matter how you start this mission, whether it's giving up TV completely for a month, or just one day a week, or somewhere in between, I suggest you stop watching the commercials with all of the hedonism, individualism, and minimalism propaganda.

In addition to eliminating television (or perhaps the Internet, depending on what you struggle with), I suggest you stop listening to secular radio. Music is a powerful tool. You know how easy it is for a song to get stuck in your head, especially if the song has a good beat to it. Have you ever looked at the lyrics to the songs to which your teenagers are listening? Those lyrics are stuck in their heads and in their thoughts. The danger is that what we think becomes reality. Most secular music talks not about love, but about lust. It talks not about loving people, but about using people. Some people believe that listening to this music is not dangerous, but I disagree.

Turn off the radio. We worship noise, and God whispers. Car rides are a perfect time for silence and solitude, a time to have a conversation with God. If you must listen to the radio, find a Christian radio station. K-Love is a wonderful station throughout the whole country. ETWN is my personal favorite station to learn about my faith. I listened to secular music growing up and through college, so the thought of listening to Christian music wasn't too appealing to me at first. Once again, we love what we know, and I didn't know any Christian music. It didn't take long, though, for me to become familiar with Christian music, and it's really good.

Those songs are stuck in my head now, and in my children's heads. When the lyrics are all about Christ, this is a good thing. What we think about we become, and when we constantly think about God, how much he loves us, and who he created us to be, we start becoming that person. My children have only ever known Christian music, and that is what they love. That is what they sing with others and to themselves when they think nobody is watching. It is a wonderful experience to see and hear your five-year-old daughter singing the lyrics, "Oh no, you never let go, through the calm and through the storm. Oh no, you never let go, Lord you never let go of me!"

Chapter Three
FREE YOURSELF

Beloved, I urge you as aliens and sojourners to keep away from world-
ly desires that wage war against the soul. . . . Be free, yet without using
freedom as a pretext for evil, but as slaves of God. (1 Peter 2:11, 16)

The first two steps to winning the war within are the knowledge
steps. These steps include knowledge of God, knowledge of self,
and knowledge of the enemy. Coming to understand God and
his plan for us helps us see the war going on around us and inside
us. After we gain knowledge of God, there's no greater practi-
cal wisdom than knowledge of self. We must know our role in
God's plan; we must know our mission in this war. We also must
know the obstacles in fighting the war. In the previous chapter, I
discussed Satan and his weapons in great detail. Satan is truly an
enemy and creates many obstacles, but the greatest enemy is not
Satan; it is our own selfish sin, since we were created with free
will. Satan has no power over us if we choose to do good—so, it's
really you against you. This is good news. This means that even
though we have chosen to fall for Satan's lies and be slaves in
some aspects of our lives, we can still choose to be truly free.

The next three steps in this war are action steps. Now that we
understand the situation, the enemies, and the allies, we're ready

to do something about it. The rest of this book will be about reversing Satan's steps. Remember he 1) removed God; 2) introduced the counterfeits; and 3) enslaved us with the counterfeits. We then must 1) free ourselves; 2) protect and defend that freedom (have a shield); and 3) revive our culture by inserting God back into the picture (have a sword).

I HAVE A PROBLEM

Step 3 of winning this war within is to free ourselves. I must warn you, this is a difficult step to accomplish. It is easy to see faults in others, but difficult to look within. It is easy to talk about problems in our culture, as we have done in the first two chapters, but difficult to act on solutions. We don't like to see ourselves as slaves to anything, and the purpose of this step is not to make you feel guilty or imply you aren't supposed to have any fun or enjoy life. The purpose of Step 3 is to encourage you to look within and be honest with yourself. Examine closely those things in this world you can't seem to do without and ask, "Am I free from this?" The first step to solving any problem is admitting you have a problem, just as the first step to winning the war is knowing you are in a war. Step 3 of winning the war won't mean much if you're unwilling to admit to your destructive habits or tendencies.

I think you'll agree one of the common qualities we share as human beings is that we all have our weaknesses—habits and tendencies that keep us from becoming saints. However, we all share the ability to improve ourselves throughout our journey. We can't claim to have arrived on this side of heaven; it's a life-long struggle. As you begin to seek out your vices and obstacles in the journey, follow the advice from Step 1 and keep your mission ever present in your mind.

THE TRUTH WILL SET YOU FREE

We cannot fight this war from behind bars. If it's the lies of Satan that have enslaved us, then what will set us free? Only the truth. Jesus says, "I am the way, the truth, and the life." (John 14:6) God made himself man and took our sins upon himself. He came to free us from bondage. Jesus died on the cross so we can accomplish Step 3. Alone, we are powerless, but through the power of the cross we can truly be set free. Jesus didn't die on the cross just to give us coping mechanisms for our sins. He came to free us from our sins.

The world says the Catholic Church expects too much. Becoming a saint is just not possible, they say, and anybody who tries to live up to these expectations sets himself up for a life of failure and guilt. If we buy into this lie, then we're stripping the cross of its power, and I refuse to do that. Christ did not die for nothing. He came to set us free, but not in the way we would expect.

Christ takes us to the heart of the matter—to the battlefield. Inside the human heart is where we win this war. Christ came to change our hearts. He doesn't free us by giving us more guidelines and rules to follow; he frees us by conforming our hearts to the truth.

Jesus says, "You have heard that it was said, 'You shall not commit adultery.' But I say to you, everyone who looks at a woman with lust has already committed adultery with her in his heart." (Matthew 5:27-28) Jesus is saying the problem isn't that we commit adultery; it's that we desire to commit adultery. Our hearts are disordered—we all seem to want to do well and be good, but it's this change of heart with which we seem to struggle. To make this point, allow me to use two very common political terms: *conservative* and *liberal*.

Many people consider themselves conservative, and an equal amount consider themselves liberal. Both sides seem to think it's a black-and-white line—that they are promoting good and the other side is promoting evil. Look at both points of view, however, and see if we can find common ground.

A person who's described as liberal may say something like, "Conservative people are so insensitive toward other people. All they care about are rules and regulations. They are just like the Pharisees, constantly condemning Jesus and his followers for breaking certain rules instead of realizing that helping people is more important than following rules. They put the almighty law ahead of mankind. They do not understand the Christian principles of forgiveness, mercy, and loving one another. All that matters is love."

On the flip side, "conservatives" may say something like this: "Those liberals have no respect for the law. They just do what they feel like doing. They try to take advantage of people who work hard and do the right thing. They promote love, but do not seem to understand what love is."

Which attitude is more Christian? Both sides are well meaning and have traces of the truth, but both have severely missed the point of what Jesus teaches us. It is true we must have forgiveness and mercy, and love one another, but we must also remember that love involves suffering. Sometimes helping people means not giving them what they want and allowing them to suffer a little. It is also true that we must respect the law—but we must also realize the law is not written in stone. Christ tells us the law is written on our hearts, where the war takes place.

If we're to be Christian, we must strive to become more like Jesus, and we can't become more like him and at the same time stay as we are. We must be willing to change. Jesus came to change our hearts. If we allow him to change our hearts so they're in full conformity with the truth, then we will no longer need the laws. We are free to do what we want, which is what the "liberals" want, and at the same time, we're following the law, which is what the "conservatives" want. Saint Augustine summed it up in one sentence: "Love, and do what thou wilt." [14] If we love others as God loves us, we're free to do things we desire to do. But without that first part, the second part is severely flawed.

I owe the following example to Christopher West, a Catholic author and speaker. I have absolutely no desire to murder my wife. I don't lie in bed at night and think to myself, "Blast those old celibate men in Rome—who are they to tell me not to murder my wife?" I don't need the law "Thou shalt not murder thy wife" because I have no desire to break it. In this sense I'm free from the law. Not free to break it, but free to fulfill it.

This is how we accomplish Step 3. We invite Christ to change our hearts. It takes an honest prayer. Perhaps there are a lot of things in our lives right now that aren't helping us become the saints we were created to be. Perhaps there are things in this world of which we just don't want to let go. Be honest with God. Tell him your desires. Let him know you really desire these things and you don't want to let go of them. Perhaps you are addicted to pornography, gambling, or a thousand other things that bring you pleasure. Let God know you desire these things, but that you want him to give you the desire to change. Ask him to conform your heart to the truth, whatever that may be. If you're honest with him, he will grant your request, little by little. That doesn't mean it will be easy, because our hearts are like cold, hard pieces of steel. To bend and shape steel is going to hurt a little bit. To allow Christ to change our hearts will involve suffering, but it's worth the freedom you will gain.

THE GREAT EXODUS

Because of original sin, we were all slaves to sin. We all had inherited a life sentence, doomed to die. However, Jesus came and paid that life sentence. He paid our bail. He has the key to our prison cell, and the door is wide open. That is the free gift. However, the gift requires action. We still have to come out of that cell. If I were to give you a twenty-dollar bill for no reason, that would be a gift. However, if you took that twenty-dollar bill home and stuck it in the bottom of your sock drawer, it would be just a piece of paper, and a waste of my money. We must use the gift if it is to bear any fruit. Using the gift of freedom means letting go of the lies, and that is hard to do.

It is simply fascinating how Jesus fulfills so many prophecies and relives the life of the Israelites. This is why we say the New Testament fulfills the Old Testament. One such example illustrates our call to freedom. The book of Exodus tells how the Israelites were enslaved in the land of Egypt for four hundred years. God came to Moses in the form of a burning bush and gave him instructions to go to Pharaoh and tell him to let God's people go. Of course, Pharaoh was stubborn and would not listen to Moses's request, so God sent ten plagues on Egypt. Egyptians worshiped many false gods, and each plague was meant to show the one true God has power over everything they worshipped. The tenth and final plague was the death of the firstborn son. God gave Moses some very interesting and specific instructions:

> Tell the whole community of Israel: On the tenth of this month every one of your families must procure for itself a lamb, one apiece for each household. The lamb must be a year-old male and without blemish. You may take from either the sheep or the goats. You shall keep it un-

til the fourteenth day of this month, and then, with the whole assembly of Israel present, it shall be slaughtered during the evening twilight. They shall take some of its blood and apply it to the two doorposts and the lintel of every house in which they partake of the lamb. That same night they shall eat its roasted flesh with unleavened bread and bitter herbs. (Exodus 12: 3, 5–8)

The blood of the unblemished lamb was a sign of the Israelites' freedom from slavery.

However, what happens when they get out into the wilderness? They start to complain about Moses (see Exodus Chapter 16). They want to go back to Egypt. They were enslaved in Egypt for so long they got used to their captivity, and actually preferred it. Egypt was still in their hearts. That is why they built the golden calf to worship, because Egyptians worshiped cows (see Exodus Chapter 32). We read this story and think to ourselves, "How can these people be so ungrateful? How can they worship false gods when they have seen the wonders of the one true God?" To answer these questions, all we need to do is look in the mirror.

Fast-forward in history to the life of Jesus, and you will see he relived this story. On Palm Sunday (the tenth day of the first month), Jesus came riding into Jerusalem on a donkey as the Lamb of God. This was the same time that the Jews were gathering in Jerusalem to celebrate the Passover as they did every year. For this yearly celebration, they would come to Jerusalem and purchase a lamb from a sacrificial flock raised for this purpose. For four days they would inspect the lamb to make sure it had no blemishes. Jesus was also inspected for four days. He was inspected by Caiaphas, by Herod, and by Pontius Pilate. On Good Friday Pontius Pilate proclaimed, "I find no guilt in Him." (John 19:6) He was an "unblemished Lamb." Then, at twilight on the fourteenth day of the first month (the month of Nisan), Jesus, the Lamb of God, was sacrificed. Do you know what that blood signified? It signified our freedom from the slavery of sin. And just as the Israelites ate the lamb at the Passover meal, we eat the Lamb every time we come to Mass and receive the Eucharist.

We are free from the bondage of sin. As the prophet Isaiah proclaimed, "The spirit of the Lord God is upon me, because the Lord has anointed me; he has sent me to bring glad tidings to the poor, to heal the brokenhearted, to proclaim liberty to the captives and release to the prisoners, to announce a year of favor from the Lord and a day of vindication by our God, to comfort all who mourn." (Isaiah 61: 1–2) Yet, just like the Israelites, we often complain. Sometimes we prefer captivity to freedom, because freedom has a price. It involves responsibility and change. The Israelites had to leave behind everything they knew in Egypt, and we too must leave behind everything we know as prisoners to sin. Just like the Israelites, we too go back to worshipping false gods every time we refuse to put God first in our own lives. What are your golden calves?

TRUE MAN

If you've never seen the movie *The Truman Show,* I encourage you to watch it. Even if you have seen it, you could benefit by watching it again. This movie is a tremendous documentary on our culture. As with most movies, I didn't catch many of the lessons the first time I watched it, but I saw it as an entertaining story. However, the more I watched it, the more I saw the parallels to the culture in which we live. I also owe Christopher West for revealing to me the connections between this movie and our culture.

The movie is about a boy named Truman adopted by a TV

producer. Truman, who was an unwanted pregnancy, is adopted by the corporation before his birth. From the moment he is born, there are television cameras on him. He lives a life that is broadcast live to the world twenty-four hours a day, seven days a week. Everyone in Truman's life is an actor, including his parents and his friends. The TV series, called *The Truman Show,* is filmed inside a studio, the largest manmade structure on the planet, which can be seen from space. Everything inside this studio is fake, except Truman. He has no idea his life is being televised and that everything revolves around him.

For most of Truman's childhood and adolescent life, he doesn't question anything. The producers of the TV show find ways to keep him on the island. When he's very young, the producers stage the drowning death of his father as Truman watches, so he becomes afraid of water. There are always news stories about planes crashing and shows calling Seahaven (the name of the "town" where Truman lives) the greatest place on earth.

When Truman is in high school, the producers try to set him up with the girl they want him to marry. However, Truman falls in love with someone else, a girl who was written into his life as an obscure classmate. The obscure classmate tries to avoid Truman but can't help falling in love with him. True love is only interested in the truth, so she attempts to tell Truman everything, but the moment she does, the producers send a man who claims to be her father. He shoves her into a car, telling Truman she has schizophrenia and that they're moving to Fiji. Truman never sees her again, but he never forgets her.

This true love sets Truman on a quest for the truth. Little by little, he starts questioning his reality. He realizes things aren't making sense. At one point in the movie, a stage light falls from the sky in front of Truman. Quickly, the radio reports that an aircraft flying over Seahaven is shedding parts.

I propose to you that in our culture, stage lights are falling out of the sky everywhere. Something is not right. It is not normal when more children are born out of wedlock than in wedlock. It is not normal when half of marriages end in divorce or separation. It is not normal for so many children to live separated from their biological fathers. It is not normal for twelve-year-old children to be obese. It is not normal for a culture to destroy one of every five children before they are born. It is not normal for TV shows, radio stations, billboards, and magazines to blatantly promote the using and abusing of human beings. We call it entertainment, when it's really tragedy.

The social diseases of hedonism, minimalism, and individualism have slowly spread through our culture. It didn't happen overnight. If it had happened overnight, we would have reacted. It is the classic frog in boiling water effect. If you put a frog in boiling water, he'll jump out. But if you put a frog in cold water and gradually turn up the heat, he will quite happily boil to death. The scary thing is my generation doesn't know anything different. This is the reality we were given. Nothing will change until we begin to question it.

There is a very interesting scene in *The Truman Show* in which the producer, whose name, ironically, is Christof (Christ-off), is taking calls from fans of the show. One caller asks, "Why do you think that Truman [True-man] has never come close to discovering the true nature of his world, until now?" Christof replies, "We accept the reality of the world with which we are presented. It's as simple as that." The next caller is the girl who fell in love with Truman. Ever since she was kicked off the show, she's been on a mission to free Truman. She begins yelling at Christof and says, "What you've done to Truman is sick. . . . He's a prisoner. . .

. Look at what you've done to him!" Christof again has a very intelligent reply (his character represents evil, and as we mentioned, Satan is a genius). He says, "If he was absolutely determined to discover the truth, there's no way we could prevent him. I think what really distresses you, caller, is that ultimately Truman prefers the comfort of his 'cell,' as you call it."

I won't spoil the end of the movie for you, but we know if Truman is ever to discover the truth, he's going to have to face his greatest fears. He is going to have to leave everything he's ever known to be true. He is going to have to come to grips with the fact that it's better to die in the truth than to live in a lie. We too must come to that reality. We too must be willing to let go of all the lies we know so well. We must be willing to face our greatest fears. We must have the courage to question what's going on around us and search for the only truth that will set us free.

ONLY AS STRONG AS THE WEAKEST LINK

I find the current health care debate in our country a very interesting moral and ethical dilemma. There are those who say the Christian thing to do is make sure everybody has access to affordable health care. I certainly agree with that statement; however, the government wants to accomplish this by enforcing a government-run plan requiring everyone to have health insurance.

Here is where the moral dilemma is, at least for me. On one hand, I want to agree that everyone should have to have health insurance. Part of the problem is that a lot of people feel they're healthy and don't want to spend money on health insurance. Then something bad happens and someone goes to the emergency room. Is it ethical for the hospital not to treat him? Of course it's not. We must treat him; it's the right thing to do.

However, now this person has a huge bill, and maybe an ongoing series of bills that he certainly can't afford. What now? Do we throw him in jail? Do we take away all his possessions? Do we just forgive the bill? If the person has just run across some misfortune, I would certainly be okay with forgiving the debt, even if I was the doctor. However, this person is now uninsurable. No insurance company is going to make money on him because he now has a chronic disability. So now we're not just forgiving one bill; we're forgiving a lifetime of bills.

Let's say we'll just help the unfortunate. So, we have a person who had an accident, and no insurance or money to pay for it, yet all is forgiven. Not a problem, except other people see this happening. They think to themselves, "I could pay a ton of money for health insurance now in case something happens, but then I would be missing out on all that money and nothing will probably ever happen to me. Besides, if something does happen, I will be an unfortunate person, and my debts would be forgiven even if I had no insurance."

So what do these people do? They choose not to get insurance. The problem is somebody has to pay for these bills. Who pays for them? The people who choose to do the right thing are the people paying the premiums and the taxes.

However, fixing the problem can't be based on forcing people to do things and buy things. The secret to curing our health care system and everything else, as I have already mentioned multiple times, is to win the war within. No system will work if people aren't willing to change. I am still waiting on a president or leader who has the courage to say, "I can't fix this problem. This isn't my country. This isn't our government's country. This country belongs to the American people. I will do all I can to lead by example, restore morality to our government, and reward good choices, but it's only the American people who can choose to end this crisis."

In this nation, we have the ability to choose what we eat and what we do. Everyone wants more affordable health care, but few look at what they can do themselves. When we consistently (not just as an occasional treat) eat and drink things we know aren't good for us, we claim we aren't hurting anybody else. When we consistently neglect exercise, we claim we're not hurting anybody else. Yet what would happen to car insurance if drag racing through the streets were legal and every person made it a habit to drag-race every day? What would happen to car insurance if there were no speed limit or traffic laws and people drove as fast as they wanted? Riskier driving would certainly mean more accidents. More accidents means insurance companies would be forced to raise premiums—for everybody.

The same is true with health insurance. When a majority of people ignore their physical health, there will be more preventable diseases. Some diseases aren't preventable, but most are. If it is constitutional to make traffic laws to keep people safe, then perhaps it is constitutional to make eating laws to keep people safe. The government sometimes seems to think they can solve every problem by creating more regulations. Is that the answer? Should we hand out citations for people who eat more than their calorie limit per day or fine them for not exercising? You know that is not the answer. We have the ability to prevent "preventable" diseases with the choices we make, so we must do our part to start preventing them. If we want to complain about the cost of health care, we must take responsibility for our own actions. We must start realizing that we're in this together, we're all brothers and sisters, all saints in the making, and we're all interconnected. We must realize that our physical health is a moral and spiritual issue. You want to serve the poor? You want everyone to have access to proper health care? Then stop trying to "get your money's worth" out of your health insurance.

Our great nation truly has the proper foundation. It thrives on freedom. Freedom is based on the ability to choose to do the right thing. It is not about being free from external restraints keeping us from doing the things we want to do; it is about being free from internal restraints keeping us from doing the things we should do. Americans are generous people who truly want to help others. We are constantly looking for ways to make sure nobody is left behind, everybody has equal opportunities, and every mouth is fed. We must return to our foundation with the belief that the best way to help people is to encourage them to make good internal choices, not force excessive external regulations.

When I look at health care, I picture how it should work ideally. People would buy health insurance from the very start of life in case something happens. They'd pay their taxes and buy insurance not just to keep their families safe, but to give others the opportunity to have affordable health care. People would eat healthy and exercise to help prevent bad things from happening. Those who fall on hard times and can't afford health insurance would get assistance from the government programs funded by those taxes everyone is paying. These people would be grateful for that assistance and would work hard to try to get off that assistance so they could one day use their own unique talents to help others in need. Doctors would be focused on helping people and not their bottom lines. They would be compensated in a way that motivates people to invest hundreds of thousands of dollars and dedicate eight to fourteen years of their adult lives in a classroom learning how to help people who are sick and injured.

Everything is focused on people trying to be the best they can be. As soon as individualism, hedonism, and minimalism enter the picture, at any stage, the system fails. Until CEOs, large companies, big banks, politicians, doctors, patients, lawyers, and *all* people stop asking the questions "What's in it for me?" and "What's the least I can do?" and stop living by the philosophy of "If it feels good, do it," our country cannot be healed.

We must stop pointing fingers. We must stop crying and start sweating. We must stop talking and start walking. We must stop focusing on changing others and start working on changing ourselves. It is an internal war that will bear external fruits. We are all linked, so it is not true that what you do in private doesn't hurt others. If you don't become the saint you were created to be, the world will suffer. If you don't play your part, it won't get played.

Again, imagine how your life would change if everything you did and everything you had were helping you to become the saint you were created to be. Imagine not only how your life would change, but how much you would influence the people around you. If what you are doing and having is not helping you become the saint you were created to be, at very best it's a waste of time.

It is easy to compare ourselves with others to justify our behavior. It is easy to say, "I'm not nearly as bad as that guy." It is easy to turn to God and say, "If you're going to send me to hell, you have to send *him* to hell." It is easy to be bitter when sloth is being rewarded and hard work is being penalized by society. Sometimes we avoid doing the right thing because of lack of justice in our culture. But it only takes one weak link for the system to fail. If the American people begin to choose self-discipline but the government system rewards minimalism, the system will fail. If the government system encourages self-discipline but the American people choose sloth and hedonism, the system will fail.

I encourage you to begin focusing within. Begin choosing to do the right thing, even if you aren't initially rewarded for your actions. Eventually, you will affect others. Hedonism, individualism, and minimalism are contagious, but so is holiness. When life seems unfair and you find it difficult to trust people, I always remember the poem Mother Teresa had hanging on her wall in Calcutta.

> People are often unreasonable, irrational, and self-centered. Forgive them anyway.
>
> If you are kind, people may accuse you of selfish, ulterior motives. Be kind anyway.
>
> If you are successful, you will win some unfaithful friends and some genuine enemies.
>
> Succeed anyway.
>
> If you are honest and sincere, people may deceive you. Be honest and sincere anyway.
>
> What you spend years creating, others could destroy overnight. Create anyway.
>
> If you find serenity and happiness, some may be jealous. Be happy anyway.
>
> The good you do today will often be forgotten. Do good anyway.
>
> Give the best you have, and it will never be enough. Give your best anyway.

In the final analysis, it is between you and God. It was never between you and them anyway.

UNWILLING TO CHANGE

The bottom line is that we don't want to change. We don't want to let go of this false world in which we feel comfortable. We make a thousand excuses and point the finger at everyone but ourselves. When I was an extern at a VA hospital in Columbus, Ohio, there was a bitter man who came in for an eye exam. I began by asking him about his diabetes and how well it was controlled. He bluntly said, "You people make me sick." By "you people," he meant health care professionals. Being a very young extern, I was a little scared, but proceeded to ask him why. He went on to say, "I know they have a cure for diabetes, but they will never tell anybody. The pharmaceutical industry is a multibillion-dollar business, and they would go broke if they started revealing all these cures so people didn't have to take all this medicine anymore."

If I had possessed a little more self-confidence, I might have challenged this cynical gentleman by saying, "I don't know of a cure for your type II diabetes, but I know of a secret alternative to all those drugs you are taking. It's called diet and exercise." A good example of this was the next patient who came in. He was well over seventy years old, had been a diabetic for more than thirty years, and had never taken a single medication for it. He controlled his diabetes completely with self-discipline and good habits.

I must reiterate my disclaimer that some people really need medication when the benefits of the medication outweigh the risks. The fact is, though, when we're given the choice between a pill and exercise, most people choose the pill. Just a few weeks ago, I heard a news story on the radio about a new diet pill. Supposedly it has been shown to work in mice. The pill tricks the body into burning calories even when the body is at rest. This is

95

exactly what I'm talking about. How much time and money are researchers spending on things such as this? This pill, even if it were to actually work on people, isn't designed to free people from their struggles with their weight. It is designed to enslave them in their vices. We are constantly looking for ways to be cured without changing our lifestyles and without self-discipline, but it can't be done. The diabetes, hypertension, and obesity are not the problem; they're the symptoms. The problems are hedonism, minimalism, and individualism.

A sentiment that is becoming more and more common in our culture is "This is just who I am. Stop trying to change me." It's preached as a form of tolerance and acceptance. For example, people will often ask, "Why can't the Catholic Church just accept people for who they are?" The truth is, the Catholic Church accepts everybody, just as God accepts everybody. Come as you are. However, you'd better not expect to stay as you are. The call of the Gospels is a radical call to change. The essence of Christianity is change. Christ is our model, and we are called to become more like him. I think most of us can agree that means we must change. The person we are today is not our true self. Who are we really? We are adopted sons and daughters of God. We are heirs to the Kingdom of Heaven. We are saints in the making.

WHAT DO WE NEED?

It is said that until you have bread, you don't understand the concept of the expression "You can't live on bread alone." Most people in the United States don't go to bed hungry. We certainly understand we need more than bread, but we've looked in all the wrong places to find what we're looking for. We are so fortunate in so many ways that we've lost the concept of what is truly a need.

Overindulgence leads to a confusion of needs and wants. As I was growing up, my mother somehow managed to get me and my three brothers hooked on the television series *Little House on the Prairie*. After my wife and I got married, I got her hooked on the show. And now my wife has my children hooked, not only on the show but also on the books—she has read every one of Laura Ingalls Wilder's books to our children. I didn't get the opportunity to listen in on all the books, but I heard bits and pieces.

In one of the first books, Wilder tells the story of her first years living at Plum Creek. Her pa has a large crop planted, and they are excited for their first harvest because they have no money. Suddenly, a swarm of grasshoppers comes, like something out of a science fiction movie or the book of Exodus. These grasshoppers are so numerous, it's impossible to take a step without crushing them. Wilder's family tries to smoke them out, but it's too late; the grasshoppers have destroyed the crops. They have also laid their eggs in the soil, so Pa knows they will be back next year. He realizes he must find another way to support his family. Pa hears a rumor the grasshoppers didn't spread more than a hundred miles to the east, so he begins walking, hoping to find work. He ends up walking nearly three hundred miles before he finds it. It takes him several months to get there, while Laura and her family wait for a letter, hoping Pa is still alive. He works for several months and walks the three hundred miles back home.

Wilder describes the season as the best Christmas ever because the family is able to afford shoes. When was the last time you had to walk six hundred miles to earn a new pair of shoes for your family? We complain so much about how bad we have it. We complain about all the things we "need" but do not have.

The fact is we need very little. I think one of the reasons I love *Little House on the Prairie* is because life seemed so simple. One of my dreams is to put in a pond and build a cabin in my backyard, a *Little House* cabin. I want to plant a garden and live off the land, and fish in the pond. I want to be a simple man with simple things, and get away from the noisy, busy world. Simplicity is the key to perfection, because the more stuff we have, the more worries we have.

We do have real and legitimate needs, but they're the very things we've lost along the way. We've traded our needs for our wants. We have an emotional (legitimate) need to be loved, but we're too busy working sixty hours a week to spend quality time with the people we love. We convince ourselves it's necessary to give our families all the possessions that will make them happy. It is certainly good to work hard and sometimes it may be necessary to work long hours, but we must keep things in perspective and not sacrifice emotional needs for material wants. We have a physical (legitimate) need to exercise and get the proper amount of sleep and good nutrition, but we're too busy. We go to the drive-through and eat junk; we stay up late doing "urgent" things; we wake up tired, so we fill our system with caffeine to function; and we certainly don't have time to exercise. Even if we do have time, we're too tired from the junk we're putting in our bodies and the lack of sleep. We have a legitimate intellectual need to learn new things and discover the wonders of the world around us, but we don't read; instead, we spend our downtime zoned out in front of the television watching shows that fill our heads with lies. We have a legitimate spiritual need to sit in silence and listen to God's voice and feed our soul, but we avoid silence and worship noise and complexity. We are constantly putting our wants ahead of our real and legitimate needs.

WHY?

Children are notorious for asking lots of questions. They have a natural curiosity—which is good—but sometimes their questions can get overwhelming, especially when they're about an order we give them. They are always asking why—why do I have to do this? We say, "Time for bed"; they say, "Why?" We say, "Eat your nutritious food"; they say, "Why?" It is tempting to give the famous response—you know what it is: "Because I said so." I can certainly relate to the frustration of having your parental authority questioned, but this isn't a healthy response. It implies you're ordering them to do things for your sake. If you're constantly giving them this response, they're going to start believing your intention is to control and manipulate them. They will see requests as hoops to jump through to keep you happy, and as soon as the opportunity arises for them to get around those hoops, they will take it.

It is best to answer their questions with another question, such as, "What do you think will happen to your teeth if you do not brush them?" or "How big and strong do you think you will grow to be if you eat only junk food?" Questions get them thinking. They may not admit to agreeing with you, but at least they will think about the consequences and understand your reasoning a little better.

Ideally, we would have the time and patience to answer all our children's questions with a series of more questions. However, sometimes a programmed response is necessary. Instead of "Because I said so," I would suggest using "Because you were created to be a saint." This is ultimately the answer to every question, directly or indirectly. Everything God created helps us accomplish this goal. Everything we have and do should be helping us accomplish this goal. If you are giving your children an order, it should be something that is helping them become saints, so the programmed response should always work. If it doesn't, then perhaps you need to consider whether you should be making the request.

This response gives your child the understanding that your only interest is to help her become who she was created to be. Whether she agrees with you or not, she should know what your goal as a parent is, and hopefully it will erase the notion that you're trying to control and manipulate her.

If you get into the habit of using this response, you may find that it goes both ways. Children are smart, and if you hold them accountable, they will hold you accountable. For example, you may be sitting on the couch one Sunday afternoon watching football when your five-year-old daughter asks you to play with her. You explain that it's the fourth quarter and the score is tied. She replies, "Daddy, is watching football helping you become the saint you were created to be?"

When we ask our children and ourselves, "Is this helping me become a saint?" we are able to more easily discern the difference between what we need and what we want. The goal of Step 3 to winning this war is to rid our lives of everything that isn't helping us become saints. Of course, this isn't easy. It involves letting go of a lot of things. Some things are always bad and should always be avoided, but I can't just give you a list of things to get rid of, because most of the time it's not the things we do and have that are necessarily bad; it's just our dependency on these things to make us happy.

Our goal is to free ourselves. Eating chocolate ice cream isn't bad. In fact, eating a bowl of chocolate ice cream with your children can be a wonderful family experience that brings you closer together. In this sense, it can help you become a saint. Eating chocolate ice cream for breakfast, lunch, and dinner, however, isn't going to help you. Before eating that ice cream, you should ask yourself, "Am I free not to eat this?" If you're eating it because your body craves it and you can't say no, then you know that it has you enslaved and you should rid your life of it.

My family members have always been big soda drinkers. My grandfather, uncle, and father all drank soda every day, like most people drink water. I rarely saw them drink anything else. Growing up, I fell into the same habit, and I really like soda. However, I know the damaging effects it can have on the body, even though we see it as no big deal compared with the "big" addictions. In fact, my grandfather, uncle, and father all struggled with diabetes, and they all died of cancer—two of them had esophageal cancer. I have to believe that the soda had something to do with that. When I see people I love, including very young children, drinking soda every day, it makes me more than a little nervous. I have successfully given up soda for periods of time, but it's one of those things I always desire. In contrast, my wife has absolutely no desire for soda, and I'm often jealous of her. It would be great if I desired only healthy things, like she does.

I use soda as an example, but the same can be said for thousands of other things, such as coffee, cigarettes, candy, chocolate, shopping . . . and the list goes on. I've seen many people who've pinpointed their problems but just can't seem to break free. Some have successfully given up certain eating or drinking habits and made great strides in their overall health, only to go back to those habits and destroy all their progress. When our bodies begin demanding certain things, we go into survival mode, and we can't seem to function until we satisfy our cravings. This makes it extremely difficult to minister to other people as we are called to do.

I struggle with watching sports too much. Playing sports has taught me a great deal about life and has certainly helped me become a better person. Watching spectator sports, however, has consumed too much of my time and emotion. I have found myself losing sleep over what my favorite team did that day. My mood often seems to correlate with how my favorite teams are doing. I have caught myself spending hours on the Internet looking at stats, highlights, and schedules of my favorite teams. There is nothing wrong with watching a game on TV, but when the game sticks with you long after it's over and becomes more than just a game, there's a problem.

Studies have shown that a male's self-esteem is correlated with the success of his favorite sports team. [15] I have no doubt this is true. I remember in grade school going to class on Monday mornings and facing my friends. I was a big San Francisco 49ers fan, and all my friends were Cleveland Browns fans. Usually, I would have bragging rights and felt like the big man on campus, as if I was somehow superior to them because my favorite team was so good. However, if the Browns won and the 49ers lost, I felt sick to my stomach and didn't want to show my face at school.

As sports fans, we seem to think we're actually on the team— we brag when we win, and start criticizing players and coaches when we lose. I remember when Joe Montana lost his final playoff game and I knew he would never play again. I was in seventh grade, and I actually cried. My mother came downstairs and saw me, and I screamed at her to leave me alone. I was embarrassed, and vowed to never tell anyone I'd cried about a football game. The only reason I tell you now is because I've seen grown men cry over sports, so I know I'm not alone. Usually with grown men, though, especially if alcohol is involved, it's not sadness but anger that takes over. I've certainly struggled with anger as well.

Even as an adult, I feel like the world is a drab and dreary place when my favorite team loses a big game. My wife called me out on this once by saying, "It's just a game." I immediately became very defensive. I told her she didn't understand how important sports were to me and how much I have learned from them. Again, we try to justify the things we love and pretend they're always good for us. We pretend they have no control over us, and we deny there are any chains. However, I've found spectator sports have sometimes interfered with my ability to be a good father and husband. Children grow up fast, and when I would skip nighttime prayers with my kids because I just had to watch some halftime show, I realized my wife was right. I am constantly trying to determine if the sports I love are consuming me. There were times when I told myself I wasn't going to watch any games that night, only to find myself unable to resist. That's when I knew I had to let go and set limits. I still love and watch sports, but I always try to remind myself there are much more important things in life.

We must become masters of the body. The soul must lead the body, not vice versa. The eternal should lead the temporal. Becoming free involves self-discipline, perseverance, and lots and lots of prayer. We need the power of the cross to accomplish this freedom; without it the task is impossible. Step 4 to winning the war, Have a Shield, is a requirement for Step 3, Free Yourself. Once we understand that Christ is necessary for our freedom, we can take action steps.

SELF-MASTERY

There are thousands of ways to achieve self-mastery and freedom. It is all about creating good habits in your life and destroying bad habits. The important thing is you practice self-discipline, not to punish yourself, but to gain custody of yourself. Researchers say it takes approximately thirty to forty days to make or break a habit. If you can go without something for forty days, you can claim freedom from that thing. If you do something for forty days, you'll feel like something is missing if you try to skip it for a day. Lent is forty days long, the perfect opportunity to free ourselves. However, you don't have to wait for Lent. Start now.

Forming good habits is not about following rules. Growing up, I followed the rules very well during Lent, as I am a rule follower by nature. On Fridays, I didn't eat between meals. I sat down to eat supper at six p.m. and kept eating for as long as I could. I figured as long as I kept eating, it still counted as supper. So around eight p.m. I finished up my supper. Then I would pass the time for four hours until the clock struck midnight, which, of course, meant it was officially Saturday. I then proceeded to pig out again. I totally missed the point, and probably ate more on Fridays than on any other day. It's about sacrifice. Sacrifices aren't meant to punish us, but to free us. If it isn't difficult you're not freeing yourself. There is no room for minimalism in this journey toward sainthood.

In high school, I was criticized at times about how strictly I followed the training rules during track and cross-country seasons. Certain foods and drinks I wouldn't even think about eating during those seasons. People would often say, "One can of soda isn't going to hurt you," or "One piece of candy isn't going to hurt you." It is true that having a small treat here and there wouldn't have hurt my physical ability to run a race, but it could've broken my will. There isn't anything wrong with treating yourself now and then—in fact, it can be good for you—however, a race is a battle of wills, and in the case of my track season, denying myself the pleasure of junk food for a period of time was a way of training my will, which I believe ultimately helped me be a successful runner.

It's not that one can of soda or piece of candy would have hurt my performance; it's the fact that having one treat is probably harder than having no treats. Pleasure isn't sustainable; it always leaves us wanting more. It doesn't satisfy our hunger; it increases it. It can slowly desensitize us to its harmful effects (if the pleasurable activity isn't good for us). If I were to drink one can of soda and it didn't hurt my performance, it would be that much harder not to drink more soda or eat more junk food. People used to point out that I might enjoy running a little more if I weren't so strict about every detail of my diet and training. I disagree. I didn't enjoy running because I hadn't mastered the ability to embrace my crosses, and I still haven't. Compromising my ability by giving in to temptation would've given me more pleasure, but less happiness. I have no regrets about what I did or how I did it. What I accomplished through self- discipline and perseverance has brought happiness, not misery. In fact, it even brought more pleasure. I assure you, a treat is much more of a treat when it is enjoyed on special occasions and not as an everyday habit.

Training my body through the sword of temperance has had lasting effects that have impacted every aspect of my life to this day. It has never really become easier and is still a constant struggle, but it is easier to recognize what I should do and can do. In a culture dominated by lust and gluttony, temperance is needed now more than ever.

THE ROAD LESS TRAVELED

We all have our own vices—things that aren't helping us accomplish our goal of becoming saints—so we all have unique journeys to make. You know your path to freedom better than anybody else. Be honest with yourself, be realistic in setting goals, and strive to achieve those goals little by little. When you slip, get back up. Perseverance will win this war. When things get hard, don't start pointing fingers and making excuses. It's always you against you. Nothing and nobody can stop you except yourself. It may be a long, difficult road, and it may involve suffering and letting go of things you really love, but one thing is certain: You cannot fight this war behind bars. Choose the road less traveled. Choose freedom.

The Scriptures remind us that being free and living a life of holiness is truly a choice that every person must make:

> If you choose you can keep the Commandments, they will save you; if you trust in God, you too shall live; he has set before you fire and water; to whichever you choose, stretch forth your hand. Before man is life and death, good and evil, whichever he chooses shall be given him. Immense is the wisdom of the Lord; he is mighty in power, and all-seeing. The eyes of God are on those who fear him; he understands man's every deed. No one does he command to act unjustly, to none does he give license to sin. (Sirach 15:15–20)

MISSION 3

Applying the Third Step to Winning the War Within

FASTING AND EXERCISE

There is genius in Catholicism. Everything is done for a specific reason. Contrary to popular belief, the Catholic Church doesn't just make up rules for people to follow. Fasting is one of those ancient traditions that many people see as outdated. The Church still recommends fasting, and requires it during Lent. Each Friday during Lent we are called to abstain from meat, and on Ash Wednesday and Good Friday, we're called to abstain from meat and fast between meals.

Again, many people now look at fasting as a hoop to jump through, and scoff at a Church that forces people to make unnecessary sacrifices. After all, the Bible says, "God desires mercy not sacrifice." To this I reply, Jesus didn't desire suffering and dying on a tree, but he did it anyway for the good of mankind. In Matthew 9:13 when Jesus says, "Learn the meaning of the words 'I desire mercy not sacrifice,'" he's speaking to the Pharisees accusing him of eating with sinners and tax collectors. Jesus is simply telling the Pharisees that having mercy on sinners pleases God much more than their vain temple sacrifices. You'll notice a few sentences later (in Matthew 9:15), when the question about fasting arises, Jesus tells them a day will come when he, the bridegroom, is taken from his disciples, and on that day his disciples will fast. God desires mercy not sacrifice, but he uses sacrifice to accomplish mercy.

Many people see the practice of fasting as too Old Testament, and even superstitious. They point out there is nothing we can do to "earn" grace. I would argue we're not trying to earn grace with this practice; we're simply trying to fulfill it. The "free gift" that God gives, the power to overcome sin, requires action to implement it. As Saint James says, "Faith, if it does not have works, is dead." (James 2:17)

It is no secret many Americans are slaves to food and drink. If we are slaves in the physical realm, our spiritual life will also be affected. To free ourselves, we need to start saying no to the body's cravings. I recommend fasting and abstaining from meat every Wednesday and Friday all year round. Now, I'm not suggesting you limit yourself to one boiled potato a day as Saint John Vianney did. I'm not even suggesting living on bread and water. I'm simply proposing that you cut out snacks and eat only healthy food. Perhaps your age, health status, or activity level is not suited for giving up food between meals. When I started training for marathons, I learned it was actually healthier to eat many small meals throughout the day to keep the blood sugar steady. I gave my body what it needed, but tried to avoid using this as an excuse to indulge in things I didn't really need.

No matter how often you decide your body needs to eat, make sure everything you eat is good for you on those days. Nobody *needs* chocolate cake for dessert. Nobody *needs* a can of pop with their meal. Drink water and don't eat junk food. Drinking water is a big sacrifice for me. I just like to taste what I'm drinking. When I was a child, I would tell my mother I was dying of thirst and needed a drink of pop or Kool-Aid, and she would tell me to drink water. I would tell her I didn't want water, and she would simply say, "Well, you aren't very thirsty, then." The same is true with food. For two days out of the week, feel the hunger pains a little bit and resist the desires of your taste buds. It will be really hard at first; it was for me. In fact, there were times when I thought maybe my wife wasn't going to allow me to fast anymore because I was so grumpy and difficult to be around that my family suffered more than I did. It is still not easy, but I've grown better at it. If you persevere, over time you'll begin to master self-discipline, and self-discipline is essential to freedom.

Another way to master self-discipline is a simple exercise routine. I recommend you set aside at least thirty minutes a day for exercise. I recently saw an interesting video by a doctor named Mike Evans called "23½ Hours." In the video, he explains how just thirty minutes of physical activity is the best preventive medicine with the biggest impact on health. Dr. Evans points out that consistently exercising for thirty minutes a day greatly reduces many health problems, including arthritis, dementia, diabetes, anxiety, depression, and fatigue. His challenge is my challenge to you: Can you limit your sitting and sleeping to 23 ½ hours a day?

There are hundreds of different ways to exercise, depending on your stage of life. For you, walking may be best. Maybe you have an exercise bike or weights, or maybe there is a particular sport, like basketball, you like to play. Many people say they don't have time to exercise because they have young children who need care. This is ridiculous. Play with your children. Exercise *with* them. In most cases, just being with them is exercise. The important thing is that you plan your exercise time and give it priority. Understand that it is a legitimate need, and should not be put off until you find time. One thing is for sure: If you exercise only when you find time, you won't exercise.

STEP

4

Chapter Four

HAVE A SHIELD:
THE CHURCH AS GOD'S HOLY HIGHWAY

*Therefore, put on the armor of God, that you may be able to resist
on the evil day and, having done everything, to hold your ground. So
stand fast with your loins girded in truth, clothed with righteousness
as a breastplate, and your feet shod in readiness for the gospel of peace.
In all circumstances, hold faith as a shield, to quench all the flaming
arrows of the evil one. And take the helmet of salvation and the sword
of the Spirit, which is the word of God. (Ephesians 6:13-17)*

The fourth step to winning the war is to have a shield. This is a good
time to point out that these five steps to winning the war are not
meant to be accomplished one by one. God is our shield, our protec-
tor, and even though having a shield is listed as Step 4, we will not be
able to accomplish any of the other steps without this one.

We access God's shield of armor through the power of prayer,
which is why prayer is essential to every step in winning the war
within. If prayer is not involved, you will never discover your mission. You will never see the war as a war, so you will never accomplish Step 1. Without prayer, you will not be able to discern the
truth from the lies. You will not see evil and the influence it can
have on your life, so you will never accomplish Step 2. Without
prayer, you can try all you want to break free from addictions and

bad habits, but you will never truly free yourself. Jesus said, "When an unclean spirit goes out of a person it roams through arid regions searching for rest but finds none. Then it says, 'I will return to my home from which I came.' But upon returning, it finds it empty, swept clean, and put in order. Then it goes and brings back with itself seven other spirits more evil than itself, and they move in and dwell there; and the last condition of that person is worse than the first. Thus it will be with this evil generation." (Matthew 12:43–45) How often do people make progress in overcoming an addiction only to fall back into the same traps? Jesus is saying that without him, we're powerless to overcome these struggles.

Getting started on the road to freedom takes prayer and courage, but staying free takes just as much prayer, and dependence on God. As soon as we feel certain we can take care of ourselves, we fall farther than before. That is why the culture says it's impossible to become a saint. Our culture has removed God from its midst, and without God it truly is impossible to be free. The lies of the enemy have enslaved us, and it is only the truth that can set us free. God is truth.

Perhaps you have often heard the saying "Come as you are to God, in all your brokenness." This is a wise saying. So many people think they've fallen so far that they can't approach God as they are. They think they need to change first from their evil ways before turning to God. You don't have to change before approaching God. In fact, you *can't* change until you approach God. However, just approaching him is not enough. In the previous chapter I discussed the importance of being willing to allow God to change us. We must do our part. Come to Christ as you are, but don't stay as you are. The power of the cross is the power to change. It is real. Once we come to Christ, we must accept the responsibility for the power we're given.

God has given us everything we need to become the saints we were created to be. The Father's mission is always to get his children back home with him. He will do whatever it takes, and that is why he sent his only son to die for our sins. That is why Jesus left the Church on earth, to fulfill this mission. The Church is a holy highway, a road to salvation. It is the only road to salvation, and this road contains everything we need to make the journey. In this chapter, I would like to use this analogy of the Holy Highway to unfold the treasures of the Catholic Church.

THE ON-RAMP

Because of original sin, we all have a life sentence; we deserve death. Original sin came from pride, and pride stems from a lack of trust in God. We all struggle with trusting God, with thinking our way could be better than God's way.

Adam and Eve fell for the lies of the serpent because they didn't trust God. Adam's job was to guard and protect his bride, yet he allowed the serpent to intimidate her while he stood there in silence. I am often tempted to look at Adam in this story and say, "What a coward!" Then I realize the story isn't just about Adam and Eve. It is about you and me. I am Adam. His cowardly blood runs through my veins. It is a cancer that's fatal to my soul. Without an antidote, without a savior, without the blood of the one who is pure, I am doomed.

Thankfully, we have our Savior. We have the blood of the unblemished Lamb of God, and through our baptism, we're adopted into this new bloodline. The most common analogy used in the Scriptures for God's love for his people is of the bridegroom and bride. Through our baptism into the Church, not only are we adopted children; we actually become the bride of Christ.

Baptism is the on-ramp to this Holy Highway. It washes the cancer from our souls and makes us new again. We go from being lost and hopeless orphans to being part of a royal bloodline destined for life in a heavenly kingdom.

THE SERVICE STATIONS

On the road to salvation we are certainly going to need some service stations and car washes, because we all fall from time to time. Baptism cleanses our souls of original sin, but they get dirty again along the journey. Reconciliation, or confession, is our service station, another piece of God's shield. In James 5:16 we read, "Therefore, confess your sins to one another and pray for one another, that you may be healed." We can say a prayer in our heart to Christ, and he will forgive us, but there's something powerful in accountability. In the Gospels, we see Jesus tell Peter, "Whatever you bind on Earth shall be bound in heaven; and whatever you loose on Earth shall be loosed in heaven." (Matthew 16:19) God gives Peter the keys to the Kingdom of Heaven. In other words, he gives Peter the power to hear confessions, to absolve people of their sins in the name of the Father, the Son, and the Holy Spirit. We also see this reference in John's account of the Pentecost: "'Peace be with you. As the Father has sent me, so I am sending you.' And when he had said this, he breathed on them and said, 'Receive the Holy Spirit. Whose sins you forgive are forgiven them and whose sins you retain are retained.'" (John 20:21–23)

In our fallen nature, we need others to help hold us accountable, because we have a tendency to deceive ourselves. Through high school and college, I painted houses and did construction in the summers. I knew some customers could be really picky about the small details, so I was very careful to make sure everything was perfect when working on somebody else's house. When my wife and I bought our current house, it was a big fixer-upper. I have been working on fixing it up room by room since that time. I have noticed when painting or putting up drywall in my own house I am much more tempted to skip the small details. Frankly, I don't care if the drywall doesn't look perfect or if there is a smudge of paint on the ceiling. When somebody isn't looking over my shoulder assessing my work, I tend to get a bit lazy. That is why accountability is so important.

In college, my roommate and I did a lot of crazy things. (Apparently, we had much more time on our hands back then.) One day, at the store, we found a product called 1000 Flushes. It is a little blue device that cleans your toilet every time you flush, and it makes the water a pretty blue color. As the name implies, it's supposed to last a thousand flushes. So we decided to put it to the test. We taped a piece of paper above the toilet and made a mark every time we flushed. We also put a big sign up that read, "Please put a mark on this paper if you flush the toilet. Thank you for your attention to this very important research." This sign was necessary because occasionally we had visitors at our apartment, and they weren't as good at remembering to make their mark when they flushed our toilet. As it turns out, the little blue thing did not last a thousand flushes. I had every intention of writing the company, but due to laziness and the fact that our research probably wasn't very valid, I didn't. (To be fair to 1000 Flushes, it says "approximate," and overall we were satisfied with the product.) Imagine if I had written a letter. Perhaps that would have held them a little more accountable for how they named their product if they had known some idiot out there was keeping track.

My point is we need to be honest with ourselves and with each other. Confession gives us the opportunity to do that. It encourages us to take responsibility for our brokenness, hand it over to God, and vow to try our best not to commit the sin again. Coming out of confession is like coming out of the car wash: Your soul feels clean and refreshed, and you protect it because you don't want it to get dirty again. Confession is a wonderful gift, and confessing often will protect us from the slippery slope of sin and keep us focused on our goal.

The sacrament of confession is not the only time we can tap into the power of accountability. We can "confess" to our friends and family as well. A couple of years ago, when our oldest child was about three years old, my wife and I started a bedtime prayer routine with our children. One thing we've done every night for the past several years is take turns telling everyone else one good thing we did that day, and one thing we need to work on. It is a powerful exercise. We are essentially accessing the power of accountability every evening by examining the areas in our lives we need to improve, what is preventing us from becoming saints. We are also celebrating our progress by bringing to mind the actions of that day that help us become saints.

By doing this activity with our children, we put ourselves at their level. We admit to our failures so they can admit to theirs. We help them understand we're on this journey with them, and that they're helping us as much as we're helping them. We are at least helping them be conscious of right and wrong, and giving them a daily reminder of their mission in life. As we pray together each night and ask God to help us become the saints we were created to be, we're ingraining this goal in their minds. By the time they graduate high school, they will have heard the prayer "Help us to become a saint" more than sixty-five hundred times. Hopefully, by then it will have become a habit, and they will continue to make this same request of God every day of their lives, long after we're gone. Keeping the goal ever present in our minds is Step 1 to winning the war within. This is just another example of how Step 4 can help us accomplish all the other steps. The more we utilize the gift of confession and get our souls "tuned up," the better able we are to make the journey, and the less likely we will run into "car trouble."

THE FUEL

The holy sacrifice of the Mass is the gas station on this Holy Highway. At Mass, we receive the Eucharist, the body and blood of our Lord and Savior, which is our fuel on this road. In his book *The Lamb's Supper,* Scott Hahn points out that blessed John Paul II described the Mass as "heaven on earth," and Hahn takes us on a journey through the book of Revelation to unfold this truth. Of course, most Catholics wouldn't describe the Mass as heaven on earth these days. Children and adolescents often complain that Mass is boring, and it seems the typical response from parents is now, "I know it's boring, but it's a family tradition, so we're going to go and be bored together."

It's funny how God works. When I was young, my mother would always drag my brothers and me to church on Sunday, and I never really wanted to go. As I've gotten older and begun to understand what's really happening during Mass, I've longed to go more often. The first year my wife and I were married and living in Columbus, we began going to Mass every morning before school. She taught at the Catholic school there, and I was going to optometry school at The Ohio State University. I have never been a morning person, but as I started getting up to go to Mass at six a.m., I fell in love with this early morning Mass. Many people don't understand why attending Mass on Sunday is required of Catholics. As I began to really experience the Mass, I realized attending on Sunday isn't required because it helps God; it is required because it helps us. Just like attendance is required at school and basketball practice to help us become the best students and basketball players we can be, Mass is required to help us become the saints we were created to be.

Everything done and said at Mass has a very specific purpose and meaning, and if you really study what's happening and what everything represents, it's fascinating. However, there are so many distractions at a Sunday morning Mass it's very hard to stay focused on these things. God does have a sense of humor, and now that I long to actually experience the Mass, my own children can sometimes make it impossible for me to do so fully. Trying to get through Mass with four small children can bring a whole new meaning to the words "sacrifice of the Mass." There are many distractions and also many people there just "fulfilling the family tradition." Some people are disengaged and just go through the motions, as if God is up there checking them off in his attendance book. I was no different for much of my life.

However, weekday Masses early in the morning are different. Every person is there because he or she longs to be there. Certain people were there every morning, and I couldn't help but notice their demeanor. One man had the build of Arnold Schwarzenegger, huge and muscular, yet he had the posture of a small child receiving his First Communion. His hands were held perfectly together, pointing toward heaven the whole Mass. He acted so humble and small in reverence for what was happening.

Often after Mass they had Eucharistic adoration in a small chapel in the back of the church. During Eucharistic adoration, we kneel in front of the Blessed Sacrament, the real presence of Jesus. We do not worship a piece of bread. We worship Christ, who reveals himself to us in the most simple and unthreatening way possible. I know the true presence is perhaps the issue that causes the most friction between Catholics and Protestants. However, Jesus makes it very clear in the Gospel of John. He says, "Amen, amen, I say to you, unless you eat the flesh of the Son of Man and drink His blood you do not have life within you. . . . For My flesh is true food and My blood is true drink. Whoever eats My flesh and drinks My blood remains in me and I in him." (John 6:53, 55-56) Many of his followers left him over that speech. They said, "This is a hard teaching. Who can accept it?" He didn't stop them and say, "Wait, it was only a figure of speech." He let them go and turned to his disciples and said, "Will you leave me too?" At the Last Supper Jesus says, "This is My body. . . . This is My blood."

There is a striking scene in the movie *The Passion of the Christ*. As the soldiers are lifting Jesus's bloody body up onto the cross, John the Apostle watches and has a flashback of the Last Supper when Jesus raised the bread declaring it was his body given up for them. Later, on the road to Emmaus, Jesus is revealed to his disciples in "The breaking of the bread." We long for Jesus to live in and through us. At Mass, we have the opportunity to become what we eat.

Protestants are so passionate about having a relationship with Christ, yet they are missing out on the opportunity to truly be one with him in the Eucharist. Catholics have the opportunity to experience this oneness every day, yet we barely make it to Mass on Sundays. And when we do go, we walk up to receive Communion like we're in the school lunch line! The more often we receive Christ, the more opportunity he has to live in us, and the more of a shield we build around ourselves for the war within. The more often we receive Jesus in the Eucharist, the more fuel we have to travel this Holy Highway and the closer we get to our destination.

However, we must be very careful in worthily receiving Jesus during Communion. Saint Paul gives us a stern warning in regard to receiving the body and blood of Christ when he says, "Therefore, whoever eats the bread or drinks the cup of the Lord unworthily will have to answer for the body and blood of the Lord. A person should examine himself, and so eat the bread and drink the cup. For anyone who eats and drinks without discerning the body, eats and drinks judgment on himself." (1 Corinthians 11:27-29)

We must ask ourselves if we are in a state of grace to receive Jesus during Communion. Jesus and sin don't mix, so unless we've truly confessed and asked forgiveness for our sins, we aren't a proper tabernacle for the living Christ. We must also comprehend and believe what we're receiving so we have the proper reverence for the sacrament.

One day in the Eucharistic adoration chapel, every seat was full, and an elderly man came in, a man I saw at church every day. Seeing there were no seats, this man in his seventies or eighties knelt on the cold hard stone floor in reverence to the Host in front of him. People like him have made my own faith that much stronger. They understand Christ is truly present. They don't act according to laws, rules, or what others do. They act according to what they experience, what they know in their hearts to be true.

Sitting in that little chapel for many hours changed me. There is a power to the presence. It is a power I can't explain, but I've felt it and long to be near it. Go to a weekday Mass and soak in the holiness of the people present. They aren't there to just hear the music (often there is none), or to listen to a great homily (sometimes there isn't one), or to meet with friends. They are there because they've discovered a great treasure—they are able to feel the powerful collision between heaven and earth. They are there to taste and see the son of the living God. The primary focus of Mass isn't the music, the readings, or the sermon. The primary focus of the Mass is the Eucharist.

I wish I could make it to Mass every day. If I were truly honest with myself, I probably could. I never regret *being* there; it's *getting* there that's the hard part. After Mass, there are times I wish I could stay there in the silence, in the arms of Christ, and hide from the world. However, it's not enough to just receive Christ. We must conceive his life within us, and bear forth that life to the world, just as a mother brings forth the life inside her. We can't keep it to ourselves. Like all great gifts, it won't bear fruit until we give it away. At the conclusion of Mass, the priest says, "Go forth, the Mass is ended." The word mass comes from the word *missa*, which literally means "dismissal" or "sending." We are sent forth into the world to allow Christ, whom we've just received with our mouths and conceived in our hearts, to work in and through us and bear fruit in the world. We must become what we eat so others may encounter Christ as well. Every day on my way to work, I've gotten into the habit of saying this simple prayer: *Lord, help me to see you in the eyes of everyone I meet, so that everyone I meet may see you in me.*

THE SEAT BELTS

Angels act as our seat belts on this Holy Highway, since they are always keeping us safe from harm. Unfortunately, just like many people don't use their seat belts, many people don't even acknowledge the angels exist. Whether we realize they are there or not, the angels are always watching over us, and each of us has a guardian angel. The guardian angel prayer is probably the first prayer I ever learned, and I still recite it every night with my children. Here is that simple prayer: *Angel of God, my guardian dear, to whom God's love commits me here. Ever this night [or day], be at my side, to light, to guard, to rule and guide.*

We have all heard stories of how people have been helped or saved by someone who seemed to come from nowhere. When I asked the eleventh- and twelfth-grade students at our parish to name some Catholic miracles, I expected to hear about places such as Fatima and Lourdes. Instead, they began telling stories of how people in their community have been helped by the angels. Each story sparked memories from other students, who then shared their own experiences. My favorite story was about a farming family. One night the parents were awakened by their six-year-old daughter, who claimed that the man on the radio kept telling her they should go down to the basement. The parents quickly got their children downstairs, and not long after, their house was totally destroyed by a tornado. The little girl did not have a radio in her room. We should thank God every day for the angels—our guardians and God's messengers.

SIGNS OF GREATNESS

You know those signs you see as you drive past the city limits or come into a town or village? They say things like "Home of the Division II State Football Champions 1993" or "Birthplace of President Abraham Lincoln"? These signs proudly display all the great accomplishments and names of famous people who came from the town. On the Holy Highway, the saints represent these signs. Depending on how you choose to look at the signs, they can give you great hope or make you feel uncomfortable. When I drive into my hometown and see all the state championship signs, I can choose to think about the state championship I should have won and didn't, or I can choose to be inspired to do something great with the rest of my life. The saints want us to choose the latter.

When I was a child, I was sure I was going to be the next Joe Montana. I wanted to be an NFL quarterback, and Joe Montana was the best ever. I studied his life, where he went to high school and college, and what other sports he liked. I knew about his family, his habits, and how he made everyone around him better. He wasn't the biggest, fastest, or strongest quarterback in the NFL, but he found a way to win. His team always had hope because he never quit. Wanting to be an NFL quarterback, it made sense to me to learn from the best.

If you want to be successful in business, study the lives of great businessmen. If you want to have a successful marriage, study people with great marriages. If you want to become a saint, you need to learn from the best. The saints are there to help us, to guide us, to coach us, and to inspire us. They are proof that the impossible journey is possible. They are proof that the world is wrong, that our goal isn't unrealistic. They give us hope and courage to attempt this journey. They form an integral part of the shield.

Again, I understand there's friction between Protestants and Catholics on this issue. I just don't understand why. Perhaps there's the mistaken notion that we, as Catholics, worship the saints and take the glory away from Christ. This simply isn't true. Most people, at some point in their lives, have asked someone to pray for them. I ask my friends and family to pray for me regularly, and I certainly pray for all of them. Why do we do this? Why don't we just ask God ourselves and be done with it? In the book of James, we read, "The fervent prayer of a righteous person is very powerful." (James 5:16) When people who are close to God pray, it has a powerful effect.

A saint is somebody in heaven who has become perfectly who God created him or her to be, somebody very close to God. The Catholic Church has thousands of canonized saints. A canonized saint is someone the Church has "proven" is in heaven. This takes many years, in most cases, and miracles associated with the person being canonized. This doesn't mean the saint performed a miracle. It means God performed miracles through the saint's intercession, or because of his or her prayers.

A saint's prayer is powerful. That is why we ask them to pray for us. I don't think bodily death prevents people from being able to pray to God. It strengthens that ability. They are still our brothers and sisters, and they watch over us and pray for us. There may be thousands of canonized saints, but I'm sure there are millions more saints in heaven; we simply have not proven it.

A common misconception is that the saints were God's favored few—that they were always saints, and lived perfect lives without the trials and temptations that we endure. Anyone who thinks the saints were always perfect should study the early lives of some of the most famous, such as Saint Augustine and Saint Francis. Perhaps we've conjured up the perception of the saints living perfect lives because we want to think they had gifts we simply don't have. Again, we hide from their journey to sainthood because if we face the fact that ordinary people before us lived extraordinary lives, then we must take responsibility for our power to do the same. This responsibility is not the curse we make it out to be. It is truly a gift. No matter what struggles you're enduring in your life, it's comforting to know that other people have gone before you and conquered those trials.

When I graduated from high school, I held five school records in track and cross-country. It took only twelve years for all those records to be broken. This doesn't take away from what I achieved. It makes it that much grander. Records were made to be broken. They are there to encourage others to aim high, and to give them confidence that it's truly possible. When trying something that's never been done, we're timid and doubtful. Just knowing that it's been done before gives us confidence. Deep down we think to ourselves, "If they can do it, I can do it."

We are all on the same team, helping each other become the unique saint God intends each of us to be. The saints in heaven are rooting for us, encouraging us to accomplish things we never dreamed possible. This race of life isn't an individual race; it is a relay race. Through our baptism, we all become part of the story of salvation history. Christ left his Church on earth to fulfill his mission. Many of our brothers and sisters in Christ have run the race before us, and now they've passed on the baton to us.

Most saints are patron saints of something. Whether you are an athlete, a businessman, a pilot, a priest, a mother, a father, or any other vocation, there's a patron saint for you. Whether you struggle with drugs, learning, chastity, addiction, or facing impossible odds, there's a patron saint for your situation. There is someone who has walked the path before, someone who has felt what you are feeling and dreamed what you are dreaming. Those people can help you, and they want to help you. Ask for their prayers. They know exactly what you need to accomplish your mission, so they know exactly how to pray for you.

Choose a few saints you can relate to, and seek their counsel and guidance. They can become trusted friends, always praying on your behalf. Personally, I've found solidarity in the saints who share my name.

Blessed Pope John Paul II is not yet canonized, but I'm confident he's in heaven. I pray to him often. He is the saint of my lifetime. He became pope exactly one year before my birth. For most of my life, he was the only pope I'd ever known. He inspired millions of young people like myself, and opened my eyes to the beauty of my faith. Much of what I've learned in regard to love, suffering, and sanctity comes from him. Much of what's written in this book was inspired by this pope's teaching.

John the Baptist is another one of my favorite saints, and I pray to him often. The past few years of my life, God has opened doors for me I never imagined him opening. He has used what I've always seen as my weaknesses, speaking and writing, to help spread his word. John the Baptist came to testify to the truth, to make straight the path of the one who would come after him. One of my favorite lines from Scripture comes from John the Baptist. When John saw Jesus, he said to his apostles, "He must increase, and I must decrease." (John 3:30) I know Christ is returning, and I know that part of my journey involves testifying to the truth. I want John the Baptist's passion and humility. I want John Wood's agenda to pass away, so that it's no longer I who live, but Christ who lives through me. I ask John the Baptist to pray for my success in this endeavor.

Another John who lived at the time of Jesus was John the Apostle, the "one whom Jesus loved," as Scripture describes him. When the other apostles ran away, John followed Jesus to the cross. He was the only apostle present at the crucifixion. He always wanted to be near Jesus, whether it was at the transfiguration, the agony in the garden, or the foot of the cross. I too want to be near Jesus. I too want to stay the course and be committed even when everything is falling apart and there seems to be no hope left. I pray to John the Apostle that I may learn his loyalty.

I was drawn to Saint John of the Cross because of his name. For the past nineteen years, I've worn a small wooden cross around my neck. I have desired to learn to carry my own cross, as Jesus tells us we must do. Saint John of the Cross was a writer, and he wrote a poem titled "Dark Night of the Soul." It describes the sometimes painful journey of the soul through this life. Sometimes we feel lonely and abandoned by God. There are days when I think to myself, "Is it really worth it?" Sometimes I simply don't feel God's presence. Saint John of the Cross helps me relate to what others also feel. As a child, I had a small wooden plaque hanging in my bedroom with a common prayer on it: *I believe in the sun, even when it is not shining. I believe in love, even when I feel it not. I believe in God, even when He is silent.* I ask Saint John of the Cross to pray for me so I will learn to carry my crosses of this life, endure the sufferings of my soul, and keep moving forward on this journey even when God doesn't reveal himself to me.

Saint John Bosco was a priest in the 1800s who inspired many troubled teens to turn their lives around and follow Christ. He won their hearts by trusting them and risking his own life for them. Saint John Bosco proved to them his motives were pure and that he wasn't trying to manipulate them or control them; rather, he was trying to help them discover their purposes.

When I moved to the town in which I currently live, I was somehow talked into teaching religion to the juniors and seniors of our parish—an idea that really frightened me. When the director of religious education asked me to teach this class, I had flashbacks to junior high, when I was extremely shy and unsure of myself. At that time, chatty teenage girls frightened me, and they would often come up to me and ask me if I ever talked—a horrible question to ask somebody. Obviously I was shy and lacked self-confidence. Teenage girls were very blunt in pointing out my weakness with this question. My face would get red, and I would start to respond, but as soon as I said anything they would point and laugh and say, "Look! He's actually talking!" How do you respond to that?

I wasn't the best student either, because I showed very little interest in what I was learning. When I began teaching these teenagers, I quickly tasted my own medicine. As a teenager, I was a closed book. I never let anybody know what I was feeling. In class, I never raised my hand; I just sat in the back and hoped the teacher wouldn't call on me. When bored in class, I gave the teacher the evil stare. I was frustrated with school because most teachers were unable to show any passion toward what they were teaching. I saw them as people trying to collect a paycheck. I was, and still am, scared to death teenagers will see me that way. I don't want to bore them. I don't know if I'm boring them—I have no idea what they're thinking.

There were, however, a handful of teachers in my twenty years of education who did catch my interest, and I try to emulate their enthusiasm. I'm still scared to teach teenagers, though. Not that far removed from those years, I know they're sitting at the edge of a cliff, about to make the biggest decisions of their lives. The decisions they make in these few years strongly shape who they become in life. I realized I had the opportunity to give them a life-directing message while they are still young, so that perhaps they won't need a life-changing message later, like most of us do after choosing the wrong path and seeking happiness in all the wrong places. The students I teach are the next generation and have the ability to change the world, but first I must convince them to change themselves. The material I teach them—much of what's in this book—is important, and quite frankly, I don't want them to miss the point because I'm a bad teacher.

I also coached high school boys in basketball for four years. Every year, I questioned whether I really had the time to be coaching somebody else's teenagers when at the time I had three small children at home. There were times when I wondered if it was worth it, and if I was really making any difference to them. Every year, though, there were situations in practice, a game, or the locker room when I felt like I really reached them, and in those moments, I knew it was worth it. Sports have taught me a great deal about life, and I've come to realize what an opportunity I had to introduce these young men to the game of life, and the part that God plays in it all. Our parish is named All Saints, and a tradition we started was praying the Hail Mary together before practice or a game, and then I would yell, "All Saints!" and they all responded, "Pray for us!" If nothing else, I've taught them those three words, and those are perhaps three of the most important words they'll ever need. I pray often to Saint John Bosco. I ask him to pray for me, that I might, like him, be given the wisdom to inspire youth.

Saint John Vianney was also a popular priest of the 1800s. He struggled immensely in his education, and was almost not allowed to become a priest. When he was finally ordained, his superiors felt he was still inadequate, so they put him under the care of an older priest. When the older priest died, Vianney was sent to be the parish priest in the small village of Ars, France. Over time, Saint John Vianney's words of wisdom, passion for reconciliation, and extreme self-sacrifices won over many souls, and people came from great distances to seek his council. He would often sit in the confessional for thirteen to seventeen hours a day hearing confessions. He only allowed himself two hours of sleep a night on a hard bed. During those two hours, he was often tormented by the devil, who assaulted him with deafening noises, insulting conversation, and physical abuse, even setting his bed on fire. Men of the parish who occasionally witnessed these encounters were alarmed, but John Vianney shrugged them off with humor. He used to say, "Me and Satan, we are old chums."

When I was in college trying to decide my vocation in life, I was considering being an eye doctor, but I wasn't totally sold on the idea. During a summer vacation to Myrtle Beach with my family, I attended Mass at a local church. Most Catholic churches have statues or pictures of some of the saints. We don't worship the statue; rather, it reminds us of that particular saint and what he or she taught us, much like a picture of a deceased loved one would. This particular church had pictures of saints hanging all around it, with quotes next to each picture. I looked for a Saint John, and upon finding one, I read the quote: "The eyes of this world see no further than this life, but the eyes of a Christian see into eternity." I remember elbowing my dad and pointing to the quote. He smiled and said, "So you think that means you're supposed to be an eye doctor?"

The quote was attributed simply to Saint John, and there are a lot of Saint Johns. It took me about three years before I finally traced the quote to Saint John Vianney. I still use the quote as my signature at the end of my e-mails. I credit Saint John Vianney with helping me choose the vocation meant for me. I ask for his prayers of guidance in my life, and to help me live a life of self-discipline and self-sacrifice.

The six saints described, along with Saint Joseph (patron of fathers) and Mary, are my trusted friends who constantly pray for me. Every morning on my way to work, I raise my shield by praying a litany to these saints. Whenever I feel the evil of the world pressing me down, whenever I struggle with temptation, and whenever I feel my children and family are under attack, I call on these trusted friends.

If Satan so much as comes near my family, I will invoke a holy war against him:

Blessed John Paul II, pray for us; Saint John the Baptist, pray for us; Saint John the Apostle, pray for us; Saint John of the Cross, pray for us; Saint John Bosco, pray for us; Saint John Vianney, pray for us; Saint Joseph, pray for us; Mary most holy mother of God, pray for us. Saint Michael the archangel, defend us in battle; be our protection against the wickedness and snares of the devil. May God rebuke him, we humbly pray; and do thou, O prince of the heavenly host, by the power of God, thrust into hell Satan and all the evil spirits who prowl about the world seeking the ruin of souls. Amen.

THE GPS

I consider Mary to be our GPS on this Holy Highway, because her role is to lead us to her son. We get to Jesus through Mary, and if we get off track in this journey she surely will be praying for us to turn around, to make a U-turn. Many people name their GPS, and I named mine Maria. One day I was very upset with Maria because I was trying to go home and she wanted to take me in what seemed like the opposite direction. I decided to trust her, and wouldn't you know it, she took me past a small Catholic church that I didn't even know existed out in the middle of nowhere. Perhaps Maria was just trying to get me to Jesus. Mary always knows the best way to our heavenly home.

A mother has a unique perspective on her children's lives. For most people, their mothers nurtured, taught, protected, and comforted them as they grew up. For these reasons, we honor our mothers. They have known us from the very first moment of our existence. The fourth commandment instructs us to honor our mother and father, and Jesus followed his own commandments.

Mary nurtured him in her womb. She nursed him, comforted him, and raised him. While we're familiar with the last three years of Jesus's life, she was by his side the first thirty years. She saw him grow into the man he became. Nobody knows Jesus the man better than Mary. Jesus honors Mary, and so should we. Honoring the mother of God doesn't take anything away from God; it shows a deeper reverence for him. Praising artwork isn't offensive to the artist. We call Mary the Queen of Heaven. Christ is King. The king has all the power, but the queen greatly influences the king.

In the Old Testament, the queen was the mother of the king, not the wife. People in the book of Kings would ask the queen to approach the king with favors, because the king would do anything for his mother. In 1 Kings 2:19–20 we read, "Then Bathsheba went to King Solomon to speak to him for Adonijah, and the king stood up to meet her and paid her homage. Then he sat down upon his throne, and a throne was provided for the king's mother, who sat at his right. 'There is one small favor I would ask of you,' she said. 'Do not refuse me.' 'Ask it, my mother,' the king said to her, 'for I will not refuse you.'"

Mary was God's most beautiful creation, other than his son. She was void of original sin because she was the handmaid of the Lord, created to conceive the Son of God within her womb. As we already discussed, Jesus and sin don't mix. Since no human being was freed from the bondage of sin until after Christ came, Mary couldn't simply ask for forgiveness of her sins before she bore the Christ child in her womb. She was made sinless by God from her conception (the Immaculate Conception) for this reason, to bring forth a savior. Eve brought sin into the world; Mary, the new Eve, brought forth the Savior to destroy sin and death. Mary and Eve are the only two women in history created without original sin. However, they both still had free will, the ability to choose sin. Eve chose sin; she chose to say no to God, which brought death. Mary chose not to sin; she chose to say yes to God, and that brought forth eternal life.

When discussing the saints, we mentioned the passage in the

Book of James that says the fervent prayer of a good person has a powerful effect. No human, other than Jesus, has ever been closer to God than Mary, and no human's prayers have ever been more powerful than hers. Jesus doesn't refuse his mother's requests. At the wedding in Cana, they ran out of wine. Mary simply told Jesus they had no more wine. He told her his time had not yet come, but he turned the water into wine anyway because his mother made the request (John 2). Notice Mary's humility in this story. She doesn't say, "Jesus, we both know you are God, and these people are out of wine, so as your mother I command you to turn the water into wine." Instead, she states the situation, and then tells the servers to do whatever he tells them. We should learn from her example. When we pray, we shouldn't bark demands at God; we should simply tell him the situation and ask for his will to be done.

Mary's will is so perfectly conformed to God's will, her prayers are never denied—they are that powerful. Mary is not only Jesus's mother; she is our mother. While Jesus is hanging on the cross, he tells the apostle John, "Behold your mother." (John 19:27) In this sentence he speaks to all of us. Mary guides, nurtures, and comforts us, and prays to her son on our behalf. What a wonderful mother. What a wonderful shield she is to protect us in the war within our hearts.

The Hail Mary is one of the most common prayers for Catholics, and it comes directly from Scripture. Let's break it down. The first line is *Hail Mary, full of grace, the Lord is with you,* from the words of the angel Gabriel. In Luke 1:28, Gabriel says to Mary, "Hail, favored one! The Lord is with you." The second line is *Blessed are you among women, and blessed is the fruit of your womb,* which is from the mouth of Elizabeth in Luke 1:42. The second part of the prayer is simply our request for her powerful prayers: Holy Mary, Mother of God, pray for us sinners now and at the hour of our death. Amen. This prayer is soothing to my soul. We are asking the most blessed creation of God to pray for us in our time of need and also at the time of our death. This is what mothers do—they pray for their children; they intercede for them.

When I was a child, I wanted to do everything my older brothers did. They would play football in the backyard, and I would want to play. They would tell me I was too little and I wasn't allowed. I would go find my mother to bring justice to this obvious situation of injustice. My mother would come outside and ask my brothers what was going on. They would say, "He wants to play, but he's too little, he's not any good, he stinks!" My mother would simply reply, "He is your brother." By pointing out this simple fact, my mother made my brothers realize they should include me in what they were doing. Now, imagine one day I die, and I come to the gates of heaven. Saint Peter is there and asks me what I want. I reply, "I want to come in." He looks me over with concern and says, "Hold on a minute." He goes to find Jesus and says to him, "We have a problem here. This guy over here wants to get in, but look at him. He stinks." I want Mary standing right there saying, "He is your brother."

Her prayers are powerful, and Jesus will listen to his mother's requests. Of course, if I don't deserve to get into heaven, Mary won't be requesting it, since her will is perfectly conformed to God's will. It is always Christ who saves us, redeems us, and gives us grace, but prayers for each other are a powerful way of gaining and opening ourselves to those graces. Mary helps us grow closer to her son and know him better. That is why we recite the Rosary.

The Rosary is one of the most powerful shields we have, and I try to keep a rosary near me at all times. Some Catholics have shunned Mary and the Rosary in recent times, almost like teenagers who fear being called mama's boys. Perhaps we fear the false perception of Catholics as worshipping Mary, so we avoid her. Yet we need Mary now more than ever. She leads us to a deeper relationship with Jesus, and in my opinion, nothing helps us achieve that relationship more than the Rosary. I recite it every morning on my drive to work.

The Rosary consists of twenty mysteries about the life of Christ. I like to think of the Rosary as Mary's scrapbook of her son. You know how mothers are with scrapbooks. My wife records every detail of our children's lives, keeping all kinds of souvenirs, such as locks of hair from their first haircut. Mary also knows all the details of her son's life, and in the Rosary she takes us on a journey through Jesus's life, from the moment of his conception to the glory of his kingdom in heaven. Each decade of the Rosary consists of ten beads, which we use to count as we say ten Hail Mary prayers. There are five decades and four sets of mysteries. During each decade of the Rosary, we contemplate one of the twenty mysteries in the life of Christ.

On Mondays and Saturdays, we recite the Joyful Mysteries, which include the birth and early life of Jesus. John Paul II recently added the Luminous Mysteries, and they are said on Thursdays, helping us focus on the life of Jesus on earth. The Sorrowful Mysteries are said on Tuesdays and Fridays, describing the suffering and death of Jesus. The Glorious Mysteries are said on Sundays and Wednesdays, highlighting Christ's resurrection and glory in heaven.

While contemplating each of these stages in the life of Christ, we say the Hail Mary so Mary will help us understand and experience what Christ did during his Passion. Mary is the only person who was there for everything. She prays we may be united with her son in these mysteries. By becoming one with Christ, we walk through his life stages in our own journey.

As I began contemplating the mysteries of the Rosary, I began seeing them in my own life. When I think of the Joyful Mysteries, I think of the joy of having a new bride and the birth of my children. The Luminous Mysteries, or Mysteries of Light, are fairly new to my life. The five events in the life of Jesus included in the luminous mysteries are his baptism, the miracle at Cana, his proclamation of his kingdom, the Transfiguration, and the Last Supper. I think of the baptism of my own children, and my new role of speaking and writing to others about God's kingdom. From the Glorious Mysteries I think of all my great achievements in life, such as winning a state championship in track, scoring the game-winning goal in overtime, and graduating as an eye doctor. The Sorrowful Mysteries are perhaps the ones closest to my heart. Not that suffering has been the largest part of my life, but through the five Sorrowful Mysteries I've discovered Christ the most. The Sorrowful Mysteries are the Agony in the Garden, the Scourging at the Pillar, the Crowning with Thorns, Jesus Carrying His Cross, and the Crucifixion. I was aware of these mysteries long before I had any idea what the others were.

I recently traveled through my own experiences of the Sorrowful Mysteries with the death of several close family members, including my father. The four months from the time I learned my father had cancer to the time of his death were a very real step-by-step experience of these mysteries. However, I first learned and discovered these mysteries while running track and cross-country in high school and college.

I never learned to enjoy running. It was always the gift I considered a curse. In every other sport, running is what we did for punishment. When we lost a football game, Monday's practice would be full of running. When we messed up a drill in basketball practice, the coach would scream, "Everybody on the line!" which meant we were going to do a running drill called "suicides" until we were convinced not to mess up the drill. But in track and cross-country, no matter how well or poorly you perform, you're going to run the next day and the day after that.

Running races became an opportunity to catch a glimpse of the five Sorrowful Mysteries in my own life. The butterflies in my stomach and fear before a race were my agony in the garden. At the beginning of the race, I would shoot off like a cannon and expend my bottled-up energy very quickly in the first half. This was my scourging. As I would cross the halfway point, panic would often set in because my energy felt spent, yet I was only half done. The knowledge of what I had already been through and what I still had to endure was my crown of thorns; it's the salt in the wound. The next part of the race would make or break me. What you do when you feel like you can do no more is how you carry the cross. That is the ultimate war within. The body cries for mercy, but the heart says to push on. I must choose to follow the body or the heart. The end of the race is just a matter of giving everything you have left. Oftentimes, once I crossed the finish line and stopped running, the real pain would begin. The lack of oxygen in the lungs, the lactic acid in the legs, and the world spinning out of control was my body's way of screaming for revenge for what I had just put it through. This was my crucifixion. My experience of running a race is just one example of how Mary introduced me to the life of her son.

Mary is a wonderful mother to us all. She introduces us to her son in a way that only she can. Her prayers and her intercession are powerful. She is a great shield for us. She is a dependable GPS on this Holy Highway, and she will always keep us on the right course.

THE ROAD MAP

We also need a road map on this Holy Highway, and the Bible serves as that road map. At the beginning of this book, I noted that the real crisis of these times is an identity crisis. We have forgotten our story. Catholics, especially, have not only forgotten the story; many haven't even heard the story! Part of our wedding vows is to not only be open to children but to raise them in accordance with the teachings of the Church. We make a similar vow when children are baptized. In other words, we promise to tell them the story. Too often, we break that promise. We expect to be able to drop our children off at church or school and have somebody else teach them. So many times we fall into the same traps as people of the Old Testament. We see the great wonders of God, but we forget to tell our children about those wonders. If we don't tell our children the story, the story is lost. If you study the readings for Mass every day for three years you will have read much of the Bible; however, this "family prayer" isn't nearly as effective if you've never really read the story.

Within the Bible is the greatest story ever told. But as with any novel, you can't just open the book to a random page and read bits and pieces each day and expect to comprehend the whole story. You may be quite familiar with parts of the story, but without the big picture, it won't make sense. The Bible isn't meant to be read from cover to cover either. There are fourteen books in the Bible which tell the story and keep it moving, and the rest of the Bible supplements that story. If you don't know the narrative and where the supplemental books fit, the Bible can seem quite overwhelming and even boring. We must learn our story. We can learn from the mistakes of past generations as well as from the successes.

Every person in the Bible is put there to act as a mirror, to teach us something about ourselves. For example, during the time of Moses, the Hebrews had been held in bondage by the Egyptians for more than four hundred years. During that time, they grew accustomed to Egyptian culture and started worshipping Egyptian gods. Pharaoh worked the Hebrews so hard they forgot their own story. They were so busy working for "the man" that they didn't have time to serve God. Sound familiar? We too have become so busy with the things of this world we've forgotten our own story. We are too busy to serve God.

God uses many recurring themes to make the story of the Bible come alive. Much of what we do in the Church today makes sense only in relation to salvation history. It is no wonder so many people claim that Mass is boring. The Mass is very scriptural, and many don't know the story. Jeff Cavins is a great theologian and author, and he has developed a Bible-study program called The Great Adventure. I highly recommend this series, because it will instill in you a passion for the greatest story ever told and make your faith come alive. Not only is the series helpful for adults to discover the story; it's also a valuable tool to pass the story on to your children. Part of our role in the story is to pass it on to the next generation. We need to remind ourselves that throughout salvation history, it was when the story stopped being passed on that people got into trouble and lost their way.

Another wonderful tool for sharing the Bible with children is the animated children's series *Veggie Tales,* which has given my children a head start in learning the stories in the Bible. There are episodes about Noah, Abraham, Moses, King David, Daniel, Esther, Samson, Joseph, Ruth, Jonah, and Joshua, as well as saints such as Saint Nicholas and Saint Patrick, and, of course, Jesus. All play roles in the Bible narrative (the saints come after the Bible narrative in the Church). They are significant to the story, and my kids know these stories within the story very well. As Jeff Cavins would say, "We are giving our children what they need [the story of salvation history], wrapped in what they want [cartoons]."

We, as Catholics, believe the Bible was inspired by God. This means it has no errors. It is not words *about* God; it is words *of* God. God communicates with us through the Scriptures. This is why Catholics read the Scriptures as a family. The fact that people halfway around the globe are reading the same Scripture verses as we are each day is comforting. What better way for God to communicate with his people across the entire world? You couldn't organize a stronger prayer chain. If you can't attend daily Mass, at least read the Scripture readings for each day. When God sends out the memo, you don't want to miss it. Imagine if the more than one billion Catholics in the world would all practice this simple daily exercise. Praying together as a Catholic family is a great shield.

Praying together as individual families is also powerful. As Catholics, we get much more out of the faith if we know the story and prepare ourselves for Mass by studying the readings before we arrive. If we don't know the story, and we don't study the readings ahead of time, it is like showing up in the middle of a movie that you've never seen before. Not only will you be confused, but you will be bored. It is a powerful family exercise to study the upcoming readings and discuss them as a family.

If we are to win this war within and keep our eyes fixed on our goal, we must understand the story that we're a part of and what role we play in that story. We love what we know. Knowing the Bible will shield us from all the distractions in this world that steal our passion. The Bible shows us the big picture, the road map of this Holy Highway.

FOLLOW THE SIGNS

As Catholics, we have a very sense-oriented religion, and we experience God's love in a variety of ways, but most intimately in the seven sacraments. We've already discussed how baptism is the on-ramp, reconciliation is the service station, and the Eucharist is our fuel. However, all the sacraments are the road signs along our journey that keep us on the road and moving in the right direction. They all make visible the invisible reality of God and help us approach our Father in heaven.

How we approach God is important. God isn't a machine or a lifeless list of laws. It is important to think of him as a friend, a father, a mentor, and a coach. Evangelical Christians have seemed to coin the phrase "personal relationship with Jesus Christ." As Catholics, we need to learn from their zeal and desire for a relationship with God. In the Catholic Church, we have all the tools, sacraments, ceremonies, "smells and bells," sights, sounds, and beautiful traditions. All provide us more opportunities to experience the collision of heaven and earth, to not just learn about God, but to physically, emotionally, intellectually, and spiritually experience God.

Yet every Sunday we may just go through the motions like robots, with no zeal and no passion. That takes the greatest story in the history of the world and makes it boring. We so often take the form of religion but deny the power of it. God can only change us if we approach him as if he is a trusted friend and loving father. We must stop falling for the lies of the serpent who tries to convince us that God does not love us. A relationship is a two-way street, involving speaking and listening, spending time together, revealing ourselves, and sharing our hopes, dreams, fears, joy, struggles, and desires.

The sacraments give us the opportunity to reveal ourselves to God, and for him to reveal himself to us. Too often we avoid getting to know God—or we avoid God altogether. Think of the experiences of birth and death. With both, we are forced to contemplate if God really exists. If God doesn't exist, birth and death are the beginning and the end. However, God does exist, and he is the beginning and the end, the alpha and the omega. Therefore, birth and death are only horizons. A horizon is nothing save the limit of our sight. Yet we live our lives as if the horizon is the beginning and the end.

In the Middle Ages, people feared the horizons because they believed the world was flat and that if they got too close to the horizon, they would fall off the earth and cease to exist. We too avoid the horizons of life. We spend the first half of our lives saying, "I want to be older." I remember my mother always telling me to stop wishing my life away, because I was always wishing for some distant time or event. Halfway through our lives, though, we start wishing we were younger, and stop celebrating birthdays because we don't want to grow any older. We try to stay as far away from the horizons of birth and death as we can. We may figure as long as we aren't near the horizon of death we don't have to worry about relying on God or even getting to know him. However, if we plan to spend eternity with God, we must get to know him now, even if death seems to be a distant horizon.

God wants us to experience his love here on earth, and to help us do that he reaches us in and through our senses. We taste and see the body and blood of our Lord and Savior in the Eucharist. We see all the colors of the Mass. The green represents ordinary time; the red is for martyrs; purple represents anticipation and preparation; white is for celebration. We see and smell the incense as it symbolically carries the prayers of the faithful up to heaven. We hear the choirs of angels and saints during Mass. We hear the bells. We hear the most beautiful sound in the world, the sound of absolution: "I absolve you from your sins in the name of the Father, the Son, and the Holy Spirit." We feel the waters of baptism as they wash away our sins. We feel and smell the holy oils of baptism, confirmation, holy orders, and anointing of the sick. Along with incense, the holy chrism of baptism is my favorite smell in the world. It represents Christian purity. In confirmation, we feel the hands of the bishop as the power of the Holy Spirit comes upon us and gives us our mission to be the light of the world. We feel the touch of the marital embrace. Marriage is a sacrament because a married couple is called to reveal God's love to the world. The goal of marriage is not to be the ultimate fulfillment for another human being. The goal of marriage is for each spouse to get the other to heaven, to reach the only ultimate fulfillment, the marriage of the Lamb. A celibate priest points us to this ultimate fulfillment in the sacrament of holy orders. By being celibate, the priest is skipping the "sign" of marriage in anticipation of the real thing. In both marriage and celibacy, we are called to the same sacrificial love as the love of the Father.

These sacraments, or signs, are all meant to keep us on the right road. The more we utilize these signs, the closer we will get to our destination.

A TREACHEROUS ROAD

Everything we need to accomplish our mission of becoming saints is on the Holy Highway, in God's Church. So many people start along this road at baptism, yet exit one by one. In recent years, there seems to have been a mass exodus from this road, especially by young people. People see exits along the way and think to themselves, "That road looks easier," or "That road looks more exciting," or "That road looks more inviting." They have fallen for the lie that life is supposed to be easy, and when they look down this road they see how treacherous it can be, so they come to the conclusion this can't be the right road. Life is hard and the road is difficult, but little do they realize that everything they need to make the journey is only on this road.

A SPIRITUAL NORTH STAR

The Church is a tremendous gift from God, a great shield in the war within. It is a spiritual North Star that always points us to true north. One night at a campfire, my older brother taught me how to find the North Star in the night sky in relation to the Big Dipper. The two stars at the end of the Big Dipper's bowl, Merak and Dubhe, are called the "pointer stars," because a line drawn between them always points toward the North Star, even though the Big Dipper rotates through the night sky.

Interestingly, the North Star played a key role in the Underground Railroad. Slaves in the South would use Merak and Dubhe to find the North Star, which led them north to Canada, allowing them to escape slavery. I was surprised to discover the North Star isn't very bright compared with many other stars in the sky and doesn't really stand out in the night. It can be hard to find if you don't know where to look. Sadly, I find this to be true of the Catholic Church as well.

The Church hasn't burned bright in recent years. In fact, she's a sleeping giant. However, for those who find her, she never wavers and is a constant guide, always pointing to truth. A lot of other stars out there seem more exciting and welcoming, but only the North Star stands its ground, even when it's not popular. It never moves. For those who discover her, the Church leads people out of a life of slavery, just like the North Star. She has freed countless people from lives of a thousand addictions. She has helped the faithful find their purposes and missions in life, which, in turn, has released them from the bondage of quiet desperation, where they're always searching the things of this world for fulfillment, but never satisfied. We need more people willing to act like the stars Merak and Dubhe to lead other people to her hidden treasure. What a beautiful gift is the Church.

It breaks my heart to see so many people who take the gift for granted, don't believe in the gift, have never heard of the gift, or simply reject the gift. Why do so many people reject the gift of the Church? I believe it is because we don't trust the Father. This religion requires us to be "all in." The road is not designed to be traveled only when the time is convenient and the sky is sunny, although this is how most Catholics try to do it. We can't be lukewarm. Jesus had some unfavorable words toward the lukewarm. "I know your works; I know that you are neither cold nor hot. I wish you were either cold or hot. So, because you are lukewarm, neither hot nor cold, I will spit you out of my mouth." (Rev 3:15–16) We must choose sides. We must be all in to travel this road, but we are afraid if we go all in with God he's going to take away the things in this world we love. We are afraid that he's going to make us do things we don't want to do. We are afraid life isn't going to be any fun, we are going to miss the party, and people will think we are weird. We don't trust the Father. Why?

We don't trust the Father because we have fallen for the lies of the serpent who tries to convince us that God doesn't love us. We all want to be happy, but the Church and the culture present very different paths to happiness. The culture says self indulge; the Church says self discipline. The culture says love is a feeling; the Church says love is a choice. The culture says go and get what you want; the Church says give all that you have. The culture says if it feels good do it; the Church says pick up your cross and follow Christ. The question is, who do you trust, the culture or the Church?

The serpent has convinced us that God doesn't have our best interests in mind and that he is trying to keep us from being happy. Nothing could be further from the truth. God is a loving Father who wants to be with his children, and he will do whatever it takes to get us back to him, even die on a cross for us. That is why he gave us this road that leads to him. If we truly want to win this war within, we will come to realize that the treacherous parts of the road are not there to keep us from making the journey, but are actually an essential part in helping us make the journey and molding us into the saints we were created to be. Embrace this beautiful gift, trust the Father, and see how God transforms you into a great saint.

MISSION 4:

Applying the Fourth Step to Winning the War Within

SILENCE

It has not been easy to hear God's voice in my life. However, as I look back at all the turning points and all the successes I've achieved, I see a common denominator that has always pushed me in the right direction. Sitting in a dark, empty church late at night; working summers painting houses at the top of a ladder; running countless miles on country roads by myself to train; driving endless miles as a mobile eye doctor in a car with no radio—all these experiences gave me the opportunity to be in silence.

A wise saying goes, "The world is noisy, but God whispers." God has never stopped talking to us. We have stopped listening. Most people feel uncomfortable in silence, but why are we so afraid of silence? Because it's there we encounter God, and we are afraid to encounter God because we know we're not yet who we're supposed to be, so we hide like a child in trouble with his parents. We know God will challenge us to change, and we're uncomfortable with transition.

In silence, we see clearly who we are, and the saints we were created to be. The disparity is heartbreaking, but it's also hope making. If we can just overcome our fear, we may catch a glimpse of our true potential. Seeing the saint inside is inspiring and can light a fire; it can give us hope that better days are ahead. I have grown to love silence. With four small children, it can be rare, but making time for it is always worth the effort.

Finding time each day to sit in the "classroom of silence" seems so simple, yet I struggle to make it a consistent habit. I long for silence, but often fail to make it a priority. When I do find silence, God never fails to show me my next challenge, idea, or dream.

We live in a world of schedules, deadlines, obligations, and duties; we are running through life falling further behind every day. There are many things I want to accomplish in life, and for the most part, I believe they're good and noble dreams. However, I'm only one person playing the roles of husband, father, son, brother, friend, teacher, doctor, author, athlete, carpenter, and coach. I struggle with finding the right balance.

In my parish alone, I've been involved in six ministries at one time and led five of them. They are all wonderful ministries, but I must be careful to manage my time. All of these ministries involve God, and he is first on my priority list. However, my family is a close second, and my career involves the care of thousands of patients, which is also important. Without some kind of guidance, I'd be flustered. God is the Divine Architect; he has the blueprint for our lives. The blueprint can be complicated and involves many pieces that must be perfectly put together to make the structure solid and stable. If we don't take the time to speak with God each day, and allow him to lay out the plans, we don't stand a chance. We will just be busy doing and having instead of becoming.

I have always been horrible at reading directions because I am too impatient. When I have to assemble something, I have the tendency to jump right in, trying to fit the pieces together without reading the directions, hoping by luck I get it right on the first try. I almost always end up putting it together wrong and having to start over, taking more time than if I would have just read the directions in the first place. My wife is good at directions, so now we assemble things together. She tells me what to do next, and I do it. The directions are important for life as well. When we don't get the directions for our lives from God first, we do things we shouldn't and find ourselves going backward instead of forward. All the wrong and unnecessary steps give us the illusion we're too busy. If you feel you're always too busy, you must ask yourself, "Busy doing what?" God is the first priority every day. God isn't just some hobby or pastime for some "religious" people. He is the most important aspect of everybody's life, whether we realize it or not.

I assure you if you just wait until you find time for God, you won't find time. I have found many things in my life. I found a five-dollar bill once. I found the missing sock behind the dryer. I even found a beautiful woman who agreed to be my wife. However, I've never found time. Just trying to *find* time for God is not enough; you must *make* time. Allow God to lead you, so you can lead others. If you choose to make time for him each day, your time won't decrease; it'll increase. I promise you. You will see who you are now, and the saint God is molding you to be. You will be challenged to change and grow in holiness. You will begin to desire the things that are worth your time, and get rid of those things not helping you become a saint.

Your mission in applying the lessons of Step 4 to winning the war within is to schedule time each day to sit in the classroom of silence. God is our shield, but he can work in our lives only if we make time for him. From this day forward, vow to set aside at least ten minutes to be in silence. Maybe it will be first thing in the morning, maybe it will be in the car on your way to work, or maybe it will be at the end of the day. Whenever you choose to do it, make it a priority.

STEP

5

Chapter Five

HAVE A SWORD
FIGHT BACK

Brothers and Sisters: You know the time; it is the hour now for you to awake from sleep. For our salvation is nearer now than when we first believed; the night is advanced, the day is at hand. Let us then throw off the works of darkness and put on the armor of light; let us conduct ourselves properly as in the day. (Romans 13:11–13)

We have discovered the war going on around us and inside us. We have extensively studied the tactics of the enemy. We have taken the proper steps to break free from the cells in which we've found ourselves. We have formed a shield around us by putting on the armor of God. Now it's time to invoke a holy war greater than this world has ever seen. This present darkness has ruled long enough. It is time to fight back.

WEAPONS OF MASS CONSTRUCTION

The fifth step to winning the war within is to have a sword and fight back. The weapons we must use to fight this war are not guns, knives, or atomic bombs. The enemy has destroyed with the swords of death, the seven deadly sins. We must rebuild with the swords of life. We destroy the culture of death by building a culture of life. We build a culture of life by mastering our own weapons, the seven saintly swords: justice, courage, wisdom, temperance, faith, hope, and love. I use this saying to remember the swords: Jesus Christ Will Triumph; Forever He Lives. In a world of darkness, these virtues bring light. We are called to live these virtues, and therefore we are called to be the light of the world.

As Catholics, we are not called to run from the culture. On the contrary, we are called to stand in the middle of the culture and live the truth. We are called to live authentic Catholic lives. Now more than ever, we need heroic Catholicism. Needless to say, we have to step it up a notch in every aspect of our lives—spiritually, intellectually, emotionally, and physically.

SPIRITUAL SAINTHOOD

Spiritually we have to become people of prayer. We have to return to the sacraments. We have to sit in the classroom of silence and listen to the plans from the Divine Architect. How is your prayer life? Do you feel awkward talking to God? The reality is we are the bride of Christ. This is the most common analogy used in the scriptures to describe God's love for his people: bridegroom and bride. The bride of Christ on earth is the Church. The bride of Christ in heaven is the communion of saints. That is why our mission is to become saints. We want to be invited to the wedding feast of the Lamb. The goal of this life is to get to know our fiancé; after all, you wouldn't marry somebody you didn't know. Our overwhelming fear of death is simply a case of cold feet.

Everything we do in this life is meant to prepare us for the next life. As I discussed in Chapter 4, everything in the Church is designed to move us closer to our heavenly destination. Just as a baby must come out of the comfort of his mother's womb to experience the life he is created to live, we must understand mother earth is also a womb, a place of preparation. We can't keep clinging to the womb of mother earth, because we were created for so much more.

The catechism of the Catholic Church is an extremely useful tool in helping us to understand our faith. It is organized very strategically into four "pillars" of the faith. The first pillar is the creed, what we believe. The creed is actually the whole story of salvation history in a tightly wound form. The story comes first because everything else in the faith assumes we know it. The second pillar is the liturgy and sacraments—how we enter the story of salvation history, and how we stay in the story as we make it our journey in life. The third pillar is "Life in Christ," describing our personal script in the story. We all have unique roles to play, yet we all make up one body in Christ. We become what we celebrate, namely the life of Christ. And finally, the fourth pillar is prayer, or union with God, intimacy with God. After finding the story, entering the story, and living the story, we come face-to-face with our destination: God.

I am convinced that the more you come to know God, the more you will desire to be with him. He is a loving Father who wants to reunite all his children in his heavenly kingdom, and his plan is always best. To become saints, we must align our spiritual lives with God. To live for God and be with God, we must first come to know God. Once we come to know God, which we do through prayer, then we can reveal him to the world. Prayer will win this war.

INTELLECTUAL SAINTHOOD

To pass our faith on to others, we must have intellectual knowledge of it, because you can't give what you don't have. To be effective evangelizers, we must study and understand the Catholic faith. One of the great tragedies surrounding the Catholic Church is ignorance, which breeds hypocrisy. Unfortunately, there are a lot of people taking the form of religion and going through the motions without passion and purpose, because they have not learned what they profess to believe. This doesn't mean we have to know and understand everything. Our faith contains many mysteries. We can't claim to understand everything about God in his fullness and totality; he is beyond our realm of comprehension. However, God does reveal himself to us, and we can come to know him more each day. We love what we know, and we must come to know what we profess to believe.

Every saint I've read about and every passionate Catholic I've met seems to have an intense desire to learn more. The Catholic faith is unique in that it never changes, yet there is always more to learn, and the more we learn, the more we desire to share. The Church is a great treasure, a gift. The gift is not designed to be kept to ourselves. It is a fire inside our hearts; if we share that fire, it will bring warmth to the world and be a means of preparing spiritual food for people who hunger for the truth. If we try to keep the fire bottled up inside, it will burn us. Evangelization is foundational to our faith, and the message of the Gospel is meant to be spread to the ends of the earth.

Evangelization begins in the home, and we must pass the faith on to our children and family members. Parents are called to be the primary educators of the faith. I am not sure if you realize this, but when our children were baptized, we promised as parents and godparents to teach them the faith, to tell them the story. Once again, every person in the Scriptures is meant to teach us something about ourselves. We can see in the story of salvation history how the people get into trouble when they forget their own story, or forget to teach their children. The book of Deuteronomy is basically Moses's farewell speech to the people of Israel as they are about to go into the promised land. His message is stern and clear: If you are going to live in a culture that worships many false gods, you must teach your children the story of the true God.

That message is as relevant today as it was back then, since we also live in a culture that worships many false gods. In high school and college, in the dorm rooms, in the locker rooms, at the parties, we have felt the temptation and been lured by the empty promises of hedonism, minimalism, and individualism. At times, I've fallen for the lies. I know that if we don't teach our children the faith or arm them with the sword of truth, they will most likely be annihilated by the culture of death, be destroyed by an enemy that doesn't sleep. I don't think parents today realize how strong the enemy truly is. The enemy wants the next generation of Catholics pretty badly and will do whatever it takes to corrupt their souls. The question is, how badly do we want the next generation of Catholics?

People often say that you can't protect your children forever. My wife and I hear this often because we decided to homeschool our children during their elementary years and they rarely, if ever, watch television or listen to secular music. We know we can't protect them forever. Soon enough they will be sent to live in the culture and they will have to choose for themselves what kind of people they will become. The war is within, and we can't fight the battle for them. That is why some good parents may raise wayward children and some wayward parents may raise great saints. However, we do intend to prepare our children for the war, training them to master their weapons of justice, courage, wisdom, temperance, faith, hope, and love. We are making sure they know the story of salvation history—God's story and their story.

While our children are young and still eager to learn, we want to give them a fighting chance to defeat the enemy they will face. To do that, we must ensure that they understand their mission to become saints. They must know their enemy and how he works. They must be free in the truest sense of the word, and have the shield of God's holy Church. They must have those swords that will pierce the darkness, and they must know their faith.

The tragedy is that many children know more about Bart Simpson, Harry Potter, or their favorite sports hero than they do about Jesus Christ or any of the saints. We love what we know. What kind of music do your children love? What kind of shows do your children love? What kind of stories do your children know? As Christians, we have the greatest story ever told. We have the greatest heroes in the history of the world. Don't let a day go by without telling your children one of these amazing true stories. Let them soak in the Gospels and the stories of the saints daily. If they don't love their faith, it is because they don't know their faith. If we don't love our faith enough to share it with others by the way we live and the stories we tell, it is because we don't know our faith. What do you celebrate? What do you serve? What do you worship? Joshua, who took over for Moses as leader of the Israelites when they entered the promised land, says this in his farewell speech: "Cast out the gods your fathers served beyond the River and Egypt, and serve the Lord. If it does not please you to serve the Lord, decide today whom you will serve, the gods your fathers served beyond the River or the gods of the Amorites in whose country you are dwelling. As for me and my household, we will serve the Lord." (Joshua 24:14–15)

EMOTIONAL SAINTHOOD

Emotionally, we must stop asking, "What's in it for me?" and start asking, "How can I serve?" and "How can I make a difference?" It is not a power reserved for a select few. We all have this power.

When I graduated from optometry school, I was excited about my career opportunity. I felt the power of being a doctor. I remember thinking, "Now I have the potential to really make a difference. Now I can give sight to the blind." Over the past six years, I've done that on many occasions. Working in the nursing homes with some very sick elderly patients, I've had many opportunities to directly or indirectly give people their sight back. Sometimes it's as simple as getting them a new pair of glasses or referring them for cataract removal. Some people have been extremely grateful, while others don't seem to care that before they couldn't even count my fingers and now they can read the bottom of the chart. I have also come to discover that many times I reach the patient too late and there's nothing I can do to cure his or her blindness. Some patients are extremely bitter and others are the happiest and kindest people I've ever met.

I quickly came to realize if making a difference means I must give sight to the blind, then my career will be a bitter failure. When you treat diseases, you win some and lose some. With the elderly, more often than not you lose. However, over the past six years I've discovered I've been given a power I never knew I had.

It's no secret that a majority of nursing home residents suffer from depression. I review the diagnosis lists of all my patients, and this disorder is a recurring theme. Treating depressed people can sometimes be a disheartening endeavor. In fact, a 2007 government study revealed the ten most depressing jobs in the United States. The first was taking care of the elderly, the disabled, and children; the second was food service; and the third was health care.[16] Now, as a doctor who takes care of the elderly and the disabled, only to come home at the end of the day and take care of four small children, according to this study I should be jumping out of a window. On the contrary, I love my job, and I love coming home from my job even more.

Why do people see these as depressing careers? I believe it all comes down to the lies of the culture, which scream that the mantra of life is about what you have and what you do. Elderly people in nursing homes have lost most of their possessions and family, so they have very little. Their physical health has greatly declined, so they aren't very active. Focusing on the lie that life is about what we do and have, they are necessarily depressed. I often walk through the nursing homes and see people just sitting there, staring at the wall with a lifeless expression. They are just waiting . . . waiting for supper, waiting for medication, waiting for bedtime, waiting to die. Completely dependent on others, they are sometimes left very bitter and angry by their state in life. This can be difficult for those who care for them.

Children are also dependent and can be very difficult to deal with at times. Days full of temper tantrums, sibling rivalry, constant demands for snacks and attention, and extreme mood swings can be overwhelming for a stay-at-home parent. The typical daily complaints and demands echoing through our house include "I'm hungry," "I'm thirsty," "I'm not hungry for that food," "She hit me," "She started it," and the list goes on.

So the common theme of the "most depressing" careers is they involve directly serving people. But if we're created to serve, shouldn't they be some of the most rewarding careers?

Because we are clinging to the "What's in it for me?" attitude, these careers get in the way of our own ambitions. They force us to let go of selfish desires. If we are always looking for our immediate reward, then we'll certainly be depressed with these endeavors. However, if we see these careers as opportunities to make a difference, and understand we were created for this very purpose, then these careers can bring a peace and joy the world rarely finds.

The power to make a difference with the elderly or with small children is enormous. Every time I see patients, I make it a point to look them in the eyes at the end of each exam and say, "It was really great seeing you today. Have a great day." For a brief moment, their eyes light up. When patients ask me what the charge is for the day, I always reply, "It'll cost you a smile," and I always receive payment. These people are lonely, and in many cases they've been tossed aside by a fast-paced world with all its focus on doing and having. The power I have to brighten their day, if only for a brief moment, is far greater than the power I have to give sight to the blind. It is a power I've possessed all along. You see, you don't have to be a doctor to put light in the human eye. It doesn't take much effort to make a difference in another person's life.

Serving others comes full circle. By allowing me to serve them, my patients give me the opportunity to meet the needs of my family and, at the same time, become the better person I was created to be. In this sense, my patients are also serving me. Their responses and words of kindness also have the ability to make my day, especially when things aren't going well. Some patients are bitter and violent, seeing the doctor as someone trying to take advantage of them. When a patient says, "It's a really great thing you're doing here; we appreciate you coming to see us," it makes my day. They are always the happiest people I treat, no matter what kind of suffering they're enduring. They each are focused on becoming a better person, not on doing and having. They understand you may be too old to do or have a lot of things, but you're never too old to become a saint. It would be nice if every time we served others we received this kind of response, but it doesn't always work that way. Perhaps we don't always see the fruit of our effort on this side of heaven.

Many of my patients suffer from severe dementia. Often I take time to explain an exam to a patient who I believe comprehends everything I'm saying, only to get a response such as, "I have three red birds." It is tempting to just say, "Forget it," especially when your efforts not only go unnoticed, but result in a less-than-favorable response. Patients with Alzheimer's disease, dementia, or severe psychological or neurological disorders can be challenging. I have been spit at, kicked, punched, slapped, pinched, and called the devil. Some patients had to be held down by three nurse aides just so I could get a peek at their eyes. There are days I would like to wear my hockey helmet to work, and days I would just prefer not to go to work at all. However, inside every demented mind is a human soul that still needs love and affection.

For many patients, all I can really do is say a silent prayer. A prayer is a powerful way to make a difference. I love walking into an elderly person's room and seeing a crucifix or rosary on the bedside table. It greatly expands my treatment options, because I know he or she believes in something beyond this life. I am not a priest, but I have prescribed praying the rosary on many occasions. One elderly lady, Mildred, asked me, in the kindest tone, if there was anything out there that could help her macular degeneration. I told her the rosary she was holding was more powerful than anything I could give her. She smiled, agreeing wholeheartedly. She was going to turn a hundred years old within the next year, and I asked if there would be a big birthday party for her. She assumed so and wanted to know if I was coming. I told her I would, and she said, "If I don't make it there, will you pray for me?" I promised I would. I did have the privilege of bringing my family to her hundredth birthday party this year, and I continue to pray for her. I pray for all my patients every night.

Whenever I treat a demented person whose mind has left him and there seems to be nothing I can do, I offer him a simple blessing. It is the same blessing I give my children each night: "May God bless you and keep you."

Perhaps the reward for these prayers is not evident in this life, but someday I hope to meet these people again. The Gospel of Matthew, Chapter 6, tells us that when we give, we aren't to let our left hand know what our right is doing. Give in secret, and your reward will be given by the Father, who sees the good that you do. If we choose to make a difference only for the people who give us the immediate reward for which we are looking, then we aren't following the teachings of Christ. Our reward is in heaven.

Think of all the good you can do with silent prayers for people you've never met. Think of the power God gives you to assist in the salvation of souls. Ponder that power and potential, and no matter what your state in life is, your life will have meaning and purpose, and you will feel alive again. Do not allow any sacrifice or moment of suffering to be fruitless. As we say as Catholics, "offer it up" for the salvation of souls, which simply means unite your suffering to Christ's sacrifice to help others get to heaven. Love is the outpouring of self for the good of others and is not self-interested. Emotionally, we have the opportunity to become saints by serving God and serving others. We soon come to realize that by serving others, we are serving God. *Lord, help me to see you in the eyes of everyone I meet, so that everyone I meet may see you in me.*

PHYSICAL SAINTHOOD

As Christians, we sometimes forget about the physical aspect of our lives and don't see physical fitness as a moral issue, or we take on the false notion that the soul is good and the body is bad. This is heresy, because the body and soul work together to help us accomplish our mission.

I have met many people who have the attitude that we should worry about what kills the soul, not what kills the body. Their excuse for being out of shape is they're not interested in living forever. They say, "You can take care of yourself all you want, but you're still going to die." Some of these people have tried to convince me on occasion that getting drunk and smoking are good because they bring people together. Their reasoning is the same: Fear what kills the soul, not what kills the body.

If we take this attitude, though, we've missed the point. In actuality, what kills the body can kill the soul. We aren't good souls trapped in bad bodies. The body and soul are both good, and they work together to make us who we are. Taking care of our bodies is essential to taking care of our souls. As Matthew Kelly puts it, "Physical well-being is the foundation upon which we build our lives. Unless we attend to our legitimate needs in relation to the physical aspect of our being, our capacity in all other areas of our life will be reduced." [17]

This means our ability to serve others is reduced. Sometimes we justify our eating and drinking habits as being noble. We say things like, "I am not afraid of my body dying; I'm only worried about my soul." The reality is, rarely do vices lead to some random day of death. I have many patients in the nursing homes who are there because they had a stroke, or their muscles and bones have become too weak, or their lungs cannot produce enough oxygen for their bodies without help. Many of them have suffered with these conditions for twenty or thirty years.

These people never imagined ending up in a nursing home, and if they could speak to you, they would tell you to let go of your vices and be truly free. Take care of your body. Many can't care for themselves because they have lost mobility, and they must depend on others to serve them. They no longer have the abilities you and I take for granted every day. It is not just about being alive or dead. It is about having the quality of life that allows you to serve the world as you were intended while you're here. Those patients certainly still have the ability to serve the world and become the saints they were created to be, but some of them bear crosses that could have been avoided with better lifestyle choices. That knowledge and regret is a huge cross in and of itself. It is a cross not just for you but also for your family, who must watch you suffer.

Many men and women in the history of our Church have been willing to die for their faith. The deaths of these martyrs inspired people to believe there is more than this life. Giving their lives was a tremendous form of evangelization. They died for the sake of the kingdom to come. However, in this day and age, in this country, we don't need more people willing to die for their faith. We need people who are willing to live for their faith. Are you willing to live? One lesson my patients have taught me is that sometimes living is harder than dying.

There is a difference between being willing to die for the faith and not caring if you die because you want to go to heaven. If a soldier were to meet his general during battle and say, "I'm not afraid to die!" and then proceed to strip off his armor, throw down his weapons, and run into the field of battle with his arms outstretched waiting for somebody to blow him away, that wouldn't be courage. That wouldn't help the cause or expand the kingdom. That would be suicide, and Jesus never called us to commit suicide, even if it is a slow suicide from a destructive lifestyle.

It is true that we shouldn't take care of our bodies just because we want to look good or because we want to live forever. The purpose of exercising and being healthy isn't to try to live forever. Physical well-being is not about counting every calorie or reading every label until you are obsessed about your life span. If that is your motivation, it won't seem worth it to you. Physical well-being is more about common sense and temperance. We know the things that are good for us and we know the things that are self-destructive. It is much more noble to choose self-discipline than self-indulgence. Choosing to take care of ourselves doesn't mean we are trying to guarantee ourselves long, healthy lives. People always have anecdotes of somebody they know who took care of themselves and died at age thirty-five. Sometimes people just die young through no fault of their own. That is the frailty of life. But if we do die at a young age it shouldn't be because of self-destruction.

The truth is, I don't want to live forever. I don't even want to live to be that old. I want to go to heaven just as much as I'm sure you do. I want to see my father again. However, deep inside I can hear his voice saying, "I've run my race. Now you must run yours. There is still life within you. As long as you draw breath, as long as your heart is beating, you must fight for the sake of the kingdom to come."

UNSEEN SAINTS

What do you do when nobody can see you, when nobody's watching? Another common cry from the culture these days is, "What I do in the privacy of my own home doesn't hurt anybody else." That, of course, is a lie. Sin is never private, because we are in this together. Let me tell you something you probably don't want to hear. What you do in the privacy of your own home has the power to help save souls that may not otherwise be saved. That is a heavy responsibility, but it is real.

Learn the meaning of the phrase "redemptive suffering." This refers to the fact that we as human beings have the power to help get souls to heaven. Many will claim there is nothing you can do to earn your—or anybody else's—way to heaven. This is true; we can't earn our way to heaven. If we get there, the only reason is because Christ died for our sins. It is because of his sacrifice that we can enter into eternal glory. Our sacrifices and sufferings are meaningless by themselves. However, when we unite our sacrifices to the sacrifice of Christ, we too can save souls. That is why Catholics bring gifts to the altar during Mass. We don't just place our monetary gifts by the altar; we are called to bring all our sacrifices and sufferings to the altar.

Christ allows us to participate in salvation history, not because he needs our help, but because by allowing us to help he accomplishes his mission of making us saints. I think the following analogy will make this more clear: I don't need my children's help to unload the dishwasher. I can unload it faster, better, and more efficiently if they just stay out of the way. However, I allow my children to help. In fact, I require them to help. Why? Because it teaches them to serve. It helps them become who they were created to be. Christ didn't just tell us how to be saved; he showed us, and we are called to imitate him.

Think of all the good you can do when nobody is watching you. I often think of my wife and all the things she does for my children and me. She once received an e-mail called "The Invisible Mother," which I believe describes her perfectly. It was written from the perspective of a mother who sacrifices endlessly with what the world sees as meaningless tasks. While raising small children, a stay-at-home mom can often feel invisible to the world. My wife is an educated woman and there is a lot she could do with her life. Staying home with our children seems like a waste of time and education to many. However, while the world may see my wife as "just a stay at home mom", I see her as a hero, with the most challenging and important job on the planet.

The mother in the e-mail compared herself to those who built the great cathedrals of Europe. Nobody knows exactly who built those cathedrals because it took so many years, and most of the workers never lived to see the completion. Some would argue that such great cathedrals could never be built at this time in history because nobody is willing to sacrifice to that degree. My wife is building great cathedrals. One day, our children, just like the cathedrals of Europe, will reveal the beauty of God's love to the world. Nobody will fully comprehend what it took to build those cathedrals, but my wife and many other heroic parents will probably tell you that their invisibility is not the affliction the world makes it out to be.

Our country has gone so far as to call the prevention of children "essential health care," as if pregnancy is some sort of disease. Children are not a disease; they are a cure for our own self-centeredness. Every parent knows that raising a child requires great sacrifice. Saints are often made in unseen sacrifices. If you offer these unseen sacrifices for other souls, you can help them get to heaven. One day you will meet every soul you helped get to heaven, and you will see just how united we all are. It doesn't matter if the world canonizes you; it only matters that God does, and God sees everything you do.

On the other hand, if you do things you shouldn't when nobody is watching—eating, drinking, and watching what you shouldn't—these things will break your will. This war is a battle of wills, and if your will is broken you are not free; you are behind bars. And you can't fight this war from behind bars. If you can't fight the war, you can't become the saint you were created to be. If you don't become the saint you were created to be, you can't play your part in God's plan for salvation. If you don't play your part in God's plan for salvation, it won't get played. If your part doesn't get played, I assure you, souls may be lost! Saint Peter tells us that the goal of our faith is the salvation of souls (1 Peter 1:9).

THE GREATEST FEAR

I know what you may be thinking: "I am inadequate for this saving souls business. I'm just an ordinary person with an ordinary job and an ordinary family. I have bills to pay and a family to feed; I don't have the time or resources for this sainthood mission." Tell that to Saint Therese, who once said:

> "You know, Mother, that I have always wanted to become a saint. Unfortunately when I have compared myself with the saints, I have always found that there is the same difference between the saints and me as there is between a mountain whose summit is lost in the clouds and a humble grain of sand trodden underfoot by passersby. Instead of being discouraged, I told myself: God would not make me wish for something impossible and so, in spite of my littleness, I can aim at being a saint. It is impossible for me to grow bigger, so I put up with myself as I am, with all my countless faults. But I will look for some means of going to heaven by a little way which is very short and very straight, a little way that is quite new[...] It is your arms, Jesus, which are the lift to carry me to heaven, And so there is no need for me to grow up. In fact, just the opposite: I must stay little and become less and less." [18]

This was the little way of Saint Therese. She became like a child so Jesus would carry her to heaven. She found a simple path and did the ordinary things of this life extraordinarily. Before she died, she promised, "My heaven will be spent on earth." She wanted to spend her time in heaven praying for those on earth. This means she will help you and pray for you. Like Therese's, your ordinary life can accomplish extraordinary things.

The truth is that our greatest fear is not of our inadequacy. Our greatest fear is of our power. In the words of Spider-Man's Uncle Ben, "With great power comes great responsibility." We must stop hiding behind our fear and start taking responsibility for the power to become saints. We read the words "do not be afraid" throughout the Bible. God wants us to understand that this mission takes courage. Fear often comes from a lack of trust, and the primary question we must all ask ourselves is, "Do I trust God?" I used to tell people, "I trust God; I just don't trust myself." This is a false humility, though. It is not about what you or I can do or what you or I can accomplish. It is about what God can accomplish through us. Our role is to surrender to God's will and trust him. God is not afraid of our sin. No matter what we've done wrong or how much we've failed, God can turn us into something great, and use us to save souls.

THE RACE OF LIFE

For ten years I ran track and cross-country, through high school and college. Before every race, I was nervous and afraid. For the longest time, I couldn't figure out why I was so afraid. I tried to think of all the possible variables, but it didn't matter whom I was running against, what the weather was like, or who was watching. It didn't matter if I was running in front of fifty or fifty thousand people, against high school scrubs or national champions. I was always nervous and afraid. Initially, I thought it was the pain I feared, because running a race hurts. Somewhere along the line, though, I realized that wasn't what I was afraid of. I was afraid that halfway through the race, when the pain settled in and my body told me to stop, I would listen. I was afraid of crossing the finish line with something more to give. I was afraid of waking up twenty years later and wondering how good I could've been if I'd tried a little harder. I was nervous and afraid before every single race because in every race my opponent was the same: me.

Ask most people the goal and purpose of running a race and they will probably tell you it's to cross the finish line first. In reality, though, the purpose is to finish with nothing left to give. The same is true about life. We find ourselves by giving ourselves away. Your life is a gift, and the gift only has value if you give it away. Don't keep the gift to yourself.

Life is a long distance race, much like a marathon. In the Olympics, the athletes in the marathon often have to run through the city streets for about twenty six miles before entering the Olympic Stadium through a tunnel to run one lap around the track to the finish. From my experience running marathons, I can tell you that there are times during those twenty six miles when you feel great, and there are times you feel like you can't take another step and want to give up. Sometimes the wind is at your back and sometimes it is in your face. Sometimes the road is downhill and sometimes it is uphill. That is life with it's peaks and valleys and it's joys and sorrows.

I don't know what it is like to pass from this life to the next, but I imagine it to be like that tunnel leading into the stadium. My tunnel will be filled with saints of ages past; the ones I pray to everyday, who inspire me, coach me, cheer for me, and intercede for me as I run my race. I will be giving them high fives as I run through that tunnel and they will be cheering and encouraging me to finish strong.

The stadium I run into will hopefully be the biggest stadium I've ever seen. It will be filled with the souls of people who I directly or indirectly helped get to heaven by leading them to Christ. It will kind of be like that movie, "It's a Wonderful Life". At that moment I will see how united we all are, and just how important it is for each of us to play our part in salvation history. Each soul we reach has a ripple effect, and that soul may reach a million more. It is my hope that my stadium will be so big and the cheers will be so loud it will shake the heavens and the earth.

After crossing that finish line in the race of life, I want to lie on the field of battle exhausted, knowing I fought the good fight and finished the race with nothing left to give. When I look up I will be face to face with my father in heaven and my father from earth. At that moment, all I want is to hear the words, "This is my beloved son, with whom I am well pleased. Well done good and faithful servant."

The thought of that experience is my deeper yes. It is what motivates me when I feel like giving up, gives me hope in the midst of despair, and is the beacon of light when I am surrounded by darkness. It is the fire inside that does not extinguish.

MISSION 5:
Applying the Fifth Step to Winning the War Within
SAVE SOULS

This chapter has discussed the infinite opportunities we have to offer up our suffering and sacrifices for the good of others. In Colossians 1:24–26, Saint Paul writes, "Now I rejoice in my sufferings for your sake, and in my flesh I am filling up what is lacking in the afflictions of Christ on behalf of his body, which is the church, of which I am a minister in accordance with God's stewardship given to me to bring to completion for you the word of God, the mystery hidden from ages and from generations past." This almost sounds like heresy. Is Saint Paul saying that Christ's Passion and death are missing something? Absolutely not. Christ redeemed the sins of generations past, present, and future. Saint Paul is telling us that we're the body of Christ. When we unite our suffering to Christ's suffering, we too can help save souls. This union is the key. Here is how the catechism of the Catholic Church explains it: "Suffering, a consequence of original sin, acquires a new meaning; it becomes a participation in the saving work of Jesus." (Catechism of the Catholic Church 1521)

Do you know what this means? It means if we offer up in prayer our daily sacrifices, we have the power to help save souls! What a beautiful mission. You can pray constantly, because God sees everything you do. You drink water instead of pop . . . offer it up! You have to get up Monday morning for work . . . offer it up! You have to wash a load of laundry or change a dirty diaper . . . offer it up! Somebody gave you this book and made you read it . . . offer it up! Maybe you wake up every day with chronic physical pain or emotional pain over the loss of a loved one . . . offer it up!

If you make it a habit to say the following simple prayer first thing every morning, your life will flood with passion and purpose: *Lord, I offer the sacrifices and sufferings of this day for . . .* You can pick any soul you want—a friend, family member, coworker, stranger, the lady who checked out your groceries, an enemy, a celebrity, a person whose name you saw on a tombstone—anybody! There are almost seven billion people on this planet and many more in purgatory who need your prayers. God desires all of his children to be with him in heaven. One hundred years is a short time to live when there are so many souls to save.

Carry out this mission any way you like, but be sure to plan your mission to hold yourself accountable. There are so many ways to choose the soul you want to offer up your day, week, or month for—be creative. Let me describe a few examples that turned out to be great experiences for me.

One day I looked up a resident of Alabama, since Alabama is alphabetically the first state. I just picked a random name (I actually just used my own name) and searched for him on the Internet. I found an address. I sent him a letter. I let him know I was praying for him and offering daily sacrifices for him over the next month so he may become the saint he was created to be. I also included twenty dollars to grab his attention. I wrote a note telling him to "use wisely" and emphasized the words "In God We Trust" on the bill. I signed the letter, "A brother in Christ."

I have no idea who received the letter, but I let God worry about that. Maybe that person needed grocery money; maybe he was at a fork in the road and didn't know what to do next; maybe he needed some encouragement or motivation to turn his life around. It doesn't matter how you choose your soul; just choose one each month, each week, or each day. Maybe someday you'll help someone from all fifty states—or all parts of the world.

Another great thing to do as a Catholic is to visit a cemetery and pick a soul named on a tombstone. Catholics believe the people in purgatory greatly need our prayers, and maybe you'll find a soul who has nobody to pray for her.

One of the most rewarding experiences I've had is a mission I call "26 Miles, 26 Souls, 26 Saints." When I graduated from the University of Findlay and ran my final collegiate track race in 2002, I promised myself I would never run another race again. For eight years I didn't run at all. Eventually I realized that even though I never felt like running, I always felt good when I finished running. I missed that feeling and knew running was good for me. An all-or-nothing kind of guy, I decided that instead of leisurely jogging (which would have made the most sense), I would run a marathon. For motivation in this endeavor, I told twenty-six family members and friends that I would offer up a certain mile of the race for each of them, and pray to their favorite patron saint during that mile that I would make a worthy sacrifice. I also asked them to pray for me as I ran their mile.

The marathon was such a neat experience the first year, I decided to do it again for charity the following year. I offered up a mile for anybody who donated to my cause and again told each person what time I expected to run their mile to keep me on pace to reach my goal finishing time. It was a humbling experience to know those people were praying for me at the exact moment I was sacrificing for them. Their prayers held me accountable and kept me going when I wanted to quit.

There are countless ways to carry out this mission. Just make sure that every day of your life is a living sacrifice. "I appeal to you therefore, brethren, by the mercies of God, to present your bodies as a living sacrifice, holy and acceptable to God, which is your spiritual worship." (Romans 12:1)

Chapter Six

FIGHTING THE GOOD FIGHT

Therefore, since we are surrounded by so great a cloud of witnesses, let us rid ourselves of every burden and sin that clings to us and persevere in running the race that lies before us while keeping our eyes fixed on Jesus, the leader and perfecter of faith. (Hebrews 12:1–2)

My intention in writing this book wasn't to provide a recipe to fix your life in five easy steps. The Five Steps to Winning the War Within are anything but easy. It's clear throughout this book that to become a saint you must be willing to suffer. When was the last time you heard a saint's story that went something like this: "Saint Bob was born into a wealthy family and grew up in a loving home. When he was twenty-four years old he won the lottery and had more money than he would need in ten lifetimes. He traveled the world, gave to the poor, and donated to some great causes. He had no enemies and everybody loved him. He enjoyed perfect health throughout his life and nobody he loved died before the age of ninety. He himself died peacefully in his sleep at the age of ninety-five." I am still looking for that story. I don't think I'll find it.

Let's get rid of the notion that life is supposed to be easy—it isn't. That doesn't mean life is not filled with joy and happiness.

Discover your mission and begin to live the life you are supposed to live, and you will discover the beauty and joy of life, even in the midst of the crosses. Saints were not the depressing and boring figures the world makes them out to be. The saints were the most joyful people to ever walk the earth. Focus on your mission, and like the saints, you will come to see the struggles of life not as a burden but as an integral part of the process. You will find a peace that can't be taken from you and does not depend on substance or circumstance. You will find an everlasting joy.

USE IT OR LOSE IT

These five steps to becoming the saint you were created to be are not a set of rules to live by; they are a way of life. It is not like you can accomplish Step 1 tomorrow and then move on to Step 2 the next day. Each step requires constant practice. Each step is a lifelong struggle and requires a life full of passion. Passion is one of those things that you must use or lose. To inspire others, you must be inspired yourself , because you can't give what you do not have. In this book, I haven't told you anything you didn't already know. The problem is not that the truth is unknown; the problem is the truth is unlived. We know the things that will help us become saints; we just don't choose them.

The *Spider-Man* movies are some of my favorite movies of all time. There are some inspirational lines in them; my favorite is at the end of *Spider-Man 3*, when Peter Parker says, "Whatever comes our way, whatever battle we have raging inside us, we always have a choice. . . . It's the choices that make us who we are, and we can always choose to do what's right."

When we do choose the things that help us become saints, they are too often short-lived. We struggle to create good, long-term habits in our lives, and we struggle to get rid of lifelong bad habits. Most people choose the road less traveled at some point in their lives. Most of us have our moments of inspiration when we choose our best selves. Sadly, those moments are all-too brief and we fail to stay on the right road for very long. When things become difficult or don't go as planned, we fall for the same old traps and temptations.

In my ten years of competitive running, it was always amazing how long it seemed to take to get into prime shape each season, and how quickly I could fall out of shape when the season was over. The muscles of the body grow stronger with persistent training over time. As soon as we begin to neglect exercising the muscles, our ability decreases.

Our spiritual muscles are the same way. God will slowly build us up if we allow him to "train" us, but as soon as we neglect God, our spiritual muscles begin to atrophy. Alone in the world, we are defenseless and don't stand a chance against the fierce enemy we face. We must have a shield from the negative influences at all times, and God is our shield. He protects us and gives us strength. He gives us every opportunity to be close to him. For so many Catholics to claim they don't feel God's presence is a great tragedy and shows ignorance of what God has given us.

Fighting the good fight requires one more essential ingredient. We must have perseverance. In James 1:2–4 we read, "Consider it all joy, my brothers, when you encounter various trials, for you know that the testing of your faith produces perseverance. And let perseverance be perfect, so that you may be perfect and complete, lacking in nothing." This Scripture verse reminds us that times of trial aren't an occasion of discouragement that should tempt us to give up, but instead are a time of encouragement that perfects us in perseverance.

The journey on the Holy Highway is a long-distance race. Saints aren't made in one day, and we can't claim to have arrived on this side of heaven. There are many battles within the war. Persevering means trusting God through good times and bad, because when we stop trusting God, we lose hope and strength. Perseverance sharpens every sword, and a dull sword is worth very little. Life with its mountains and valleys is similar to sports, and it's important not to get too high after a win or too low after a loss. If success comes our way, we must remember that we are not responsible for making it happen. God deserves all the credit. When success breeds confidence, we must maintain humility. When failures come our way and we're humbled, we must maintain confidence and trust that God has a plan. We must never give up. "Let us not grow tired of doing good, for in due time we shall reap our harvest, if we do not give up." (Galatians 6:9)

GOT TO HAVE FAITH

Saint Augustine once said, "Faith is to believe what we do not see, and the reward of this faith is to see what we believe." Faith is the sword that destroys fear and self-doubt. It also provides evidence of what we can't see with our eyes. Sight is what we see with our eyes, and vision is what we see with our mind. Faith requires great vision.

An experience that has taught me a great deal about faith began when my wife and I bought our house, which, as I've mentioned, was in really bad shape. I had just graduated from optometry school, I didn't have a job yet, we were expecting our second child, and we had very little money. We didn't want to rent anymore, so we found a house in the location we wanted (out in the country) and within our budget, which was not easy to do. The house was a foreclosure, so when we walked through for the first time, it didn't look very good. The kitchen cabinets were gone. There was no kitchen sink. There were two bedrooms on the main floor, and only one had carpet and finished drywall. There were three bedrooms upstairs, all torn apart, none finished. The basement was unfinished. It had a lot of space with poured concrete walls and floors, but wires were hanging from the ceiling and the floor was extremely unlevel. The toilet and sink in the bathroom were stained orange from all the rust in the water. The shingles were falling off the roof; one area had a gaping hole. We had the radon levels tested, and the man who did the testing reported he had been doing his job for twenty years and had never seen levels as high as they were in this house.

The man who appraised the house said, "I will appraise it for what the bank is trying to sell it to you for, but I'm telling you now, if you don't fix the roof right away, the house will be worth nothing by the end of the summer because it will be covered with black mold." I wasn't fazed; I planned on fixing the roof right away. Then, I had a contractor come in to give me an estimate to fix up the house. He really didn't want to give me any numbers; he just kept telling me it wasn't worth it. "There is too much stuff messed up. Nothing is straight. Who knows what's hidden behind these walls?"

I didn't listen to him. I didn't see the uneven floors, the holes in the roof, the empty kitchen, the bare basement, or the unfinished bedrooms. I saw potential and a solid foundation. I had a little construction experience from my college years and believed I could fix up the house myself, so we bought it and began fixing it up one step at a time, starting with the roof.

It has been a long, slow process over the past five years, but little by little we've transformed each room in the house. Every room presented new challenges, new doubts, and more questions about the decision to buy the house. Every room thus far has been conquered. The financial value of the house has almost doubled in five years, but the sentimental value is priceless. The more we've worked on the house, the more we've felt it's really ours, and I am proud of what we've accomplished. We have all the before and after pictures in a slide show, and we play it for our friends when they come over.

It is not perfect. We really just learned as we went. I had to patch a lot of stuff and there are still some uneven floors and funny-looking walls, but the foundation is strong. It is home. It is our home. We saved it. Without us, it would have perished. We revived it. My goal has never been to just make it livable. I didn't want a house; I wanted a home. I have big dreams for this home. With all the work and effort we've put into saving this house, we've grown quite attached to it. Even if we were to win a million dollars today, I don't think we would leave this house.

So what does this all have to do with faith? As human beings, we've all messed up and have the scars of sin—our own holes in the roof, unfinished rooms, high radon levels, and uneven walls and floors. Does God ever look at us in all our brokenness and think we aren't worth saving? Despite all our faults and imperfections, God chose to save us, even though he knew it wouldn't be easy. It would've been easier to just wipe us out and start over like in the days of Noah, but God chose a different path of salvation.

After all he went through to save our souls, he will never abandon us. He has invested too much into saving us. He fixes us up even though it isn't easy. In an ongoing process, he patiently continues to work on changing our hearts. The changes he must make to transform us into saints are often drastic and painful. Our scars from the past aren't the prettiest things. However, scar tissue is stronger than the original tissue and reminds us where we've been and how far we've come. God doesn't just want to make a house out of us. He wants to make us into a home in which he can live.

He doesn't see the sinners we are; he sees the saints inside. By virtue of baptism, we have a strong foundation to build upon.

I have faith God will never abandon me. No matter how grim things look, I will not lose faith. Even if the sky is falling, I will still have faith that God will save me. Faith is an essential sword in fighting this war; as Blessed Mother Teresa of Calcutta once said, "God has not called me to be successful; he has called me to be faithful."

JUST PUSH

There are many times in life when we develop the attitude of "Why bother?" We've all experienced times when we've put our heart and soul into something, and it just didn't work out the way we wanted. Maybe we try to share our enthusiasm and passion with others, and nobody seems to care. Inspiring people is difficult and takes patience. It is as if you have a great gift and you can't help but want to share it, but nobody will take it. We have to remember that it's God who changes people. No matter how hard we try, we can't truly give people the gift; we can only point them toward it. They must choose.

Everyone is on a different part of the journey, and sometimes you can't reach them right away. It is important to persevere, to stay the course and never give up hope. Maybe we spend countless hours working, studying, praying, practicing, or training only to end up failing, which is frustrating.

There was a point in my college track career when I was very frustrated because I kept running the same time over and over. Through the course of an entire track season, my best and worst times in the 800m race differed by less than a half a second. No matter how hard I trained and practiced, I just couldn't seem to get any better. One day that season, I received a random e-mail that had been forwarded many times. The e-mail was called "Just Push." The letters in the word *push* stand for Pray Until Something Happens. The story goes like this:

> A man was sleeping at night in his cabin when suddenly his room filled with light, and God appeared. The Lord told the man he had work for him to do, and showed him a large rock in front of his cabin. The Lord explained that the man was to push against the rock with all his might. So this the man did, day after day. For many years he toiled from sunup to sundown, his shoulders set squarely against the cold, massive surface of the unmoving rock, pushing with all his might. Each night the man returned to his cabin sore and worn out, feeling that his whole day had been spent in vain. Since the man was showing discouragement, the Adversary (Satan) decided to enter the picture by placing thoughts into his weary mind: "You have been pushing against that rock for a long time, and it hasn't moved," thus giving the man the impression that the task was impossible and that he was a failure. These thoughts discouraged and disheartened the man.
>
> "Why should I kill myself over this?" he thought. "I'll just put in my time, giving just the minimum effort, and that will be good enough." And that is what he planned to do, until one day he decided to make it a matter of prayer and take his troubled thoughts to the Lord. "Lord," he said, "I have labored long and hard in your service, putting all my strength to do that which you have asked. Yet, after all this time, I have not even budged that rock by half a millimeter. What is wrong? Why am I failing?"
>
> The Lord responded compassionately, "My friend, when I asked you to serve me and you accepted, I told you that

your task was to push against the rock with all of your strength, which you have done. Never once did I mention to you that I expected you to move it. Your task was to push. And now you come to me with your strength spent, thinking that you have failed. But is that really so? Look at yourself. Your arms are strong and muscled, your back sinewy and brown, your hands are callused from constant pressure, and your legs have become massive and hard. Through opposition you have grown much, and your abilities now surpass that which you used to have. Yet you haven't moved the rock. But your calling was to be obedient and to push and to exercise your faith and trust in my wisdom. This you have done. Now I, my friend, will move the rock."

I realized life isn't about reaching all our goals. It is about pursuing them. This life is the journey; the destination can only be reached in the kingdom to come. It is through resistance that we're made strong, and it is not supposed to be easy.

TAKING ACTION

Actions will always speak louder than words. People may doubt what you say, but they'll always believe what you do. It is time to put on the shield of armor and unsheathe the swords. God's holy Church is under attack. The Church is the bride of Christ, and that bride carries within her a new life. We must fight to defend and protect that life with all our might, as a husband would defend and protect his bride and unborn child from any harm.

Throughout this book I have given you several missions and action steps to help you win this war within. To help you accomplish Step 1, I encouraged you to write the words "Become a saint" on several pieces of paper and post them in locations where you'll see them throughout the day to remind you of your goal. To help accomplish Step 2, start watching the "game film" of the enemy to recognize hedonism, minimalism, and individualism in your own life and in the culture around you. Unplug from the world that's constantly trying to sell you this counterfeit lifestyle. Step 3 can be mastered through self-discipline, prayer, and fasting. Step 4 is the key to every step. Get into the habit of spending ten minutes every day speaking and listening to God. Befriend silence, and receive the plan for your life from the Divine Architect. Step 5 is all about saving souls by mastering the virtues. Go out into the world and make a difference. Be a soldier in God's army. Encourage someone. Write a letter. Visit a cemetery. Make a sacrifice. Offer it up. Learn patience. Teach a child. Learn from a child. Smile at someone. Be sincere. Stop pretending. Live life with passion. Pray for your friends, family, Church, and nation. Pray for strangers and your enemies. Pray constantly.

It is time to take action. You can't expect anyone to do something you aren't willing to do yourself. If you aren't free, you can't expect your children to be free. So often I catch myself sneaking around the snack cupboard trying to get an extra treat while my children aren't looking, because I'm constantly telling them too many snacks and treats aren't good for them. They hold me accountable as well. Don't tell them it's okay for you because you're an adult. Hold yourself to the same standards you hold them. There is no good lesson in teaching them that one day they can indulge too. If you want them to be disciplined, be disciplined. If you want them to become saints, become a saint. Don't just tell them; show them.

THE OPPORTUNITY AT HAND

We are in crisis as a nation and as a Church. However, more than a crisis, I see an opportunity. During times of crisis the soil is most fertile for the seeds of conversion. Now, maybe more than ever, people are searching for the truth. Your family, friends, coworkers, and random people who pass through your life are all looking for truth. The question is, will they find it? People yearn to live an authentic life. Show them how. Deep down inside, the people in your life all want to be saints; they just don't know how. If you would just lead them, they would follow you. Your mission is to become a saint. To do that, you must focus on saving souls, and saving souls is a beautiful mission.

AWAKEN THE SLEEPING GIANT

Let's return to the quote from John Paul II in the introduction: "We are now standing in the face of the greatest historical confrontation humanity has ever experienced. I do not think the wide circle of the American society, or the wide circle of the Christian community realize this fully. We are now facing the final confrontation between the Church and the antichurch, between the Gospel and the antigospel, between Christ and the antichrist. This confrontation lies within the plans of divine providence. It is, therefore, in God's plan, and it must be a trial which the Church must take up, and face courageously."

We see a lot of people going through the motions, following a list of rules and regulations. Some are sitting at Mass on Sunday expecting God to check them off in the attendance book. Others are just trying to get by and survive. People are chained by lives of a thousand addictions. An attitude of defeat and acceptance of a culture of death prevails. There is complacency with being ordinary. But most of all, we see fear. For the first thirty years of my life, I allowed fear to be my dominant emotion, and I don't want to do that anymore.

Out of the darkness, there will come a great light. I have hope that something big is about to happen. Recently I took my children fishing for the first time. I hadn't been fishing since I was a child. For a long time we couldn't catch anything. Their excitement quickly turned to frustration, which quickly turned to boredom. Suddenly, there was a nibble on the line. As I helped my daughter hold her fishing pole, we felt the tug on the end of the line and saw the bobber moving. That tug on the line brought a new excitement, almost a jolt of electricity. Moments earlier, nothing had been there, but now something was definitely in there. It was alive. Finally, we hooked a fish and felt it fight as we reeled it in. I will never forget the excitement on my daughter's face and the sound of her laugh as she held that fish on the end of her pole.

For many years, the waters have seemed empty for the Church. It has seemed that there's little life. Suddenly, I feel the tug. I feel the jolt. It is real, alive, and exciting. It is what Peter Kreeft referred to as "Jesus Shock." Once you feel the tug, it can't possibly be boring, because something big is about to happen. A revival is on the horizon. Seminarians are on fire for fighting this war. Good priests are willing to speak the truth no matter how much they are persecuted, no matter how difficult the truth may be. Strong families are building God's kingdom one child at a time. The Church is on the verge of reawakening, and I want to be a part of it. I don't want to just sit back, watch, and wait. I want to be a pioneer in helping to awaken the sleeping giant called the Church.

As an eye doctor, it's my vocation in life to help people see the world more clearly. However, as a disciple of Christ, part of my mission in life is helping people see the truth more clearly. This world may be in darkness, but the Church is the light. We are the light of the world.

Remember, the goal isn't just to finish the race of life, but to finish the race with nothing left to give. I hope you will join me and let your light shine. The baton is in your hands, so run your race. You have been given a gift; do not keep it to yourself. To fulfill its purpose, you must give it away. Let me leave you with this quote from Saint Catherine of Siena: "If you are what you should be, you will set the whole world ablaze!" Become what you should be. Become a saint.

ABOUT THE AUTHOR

Dr. John R. Wood grew up in southwest Ohio where he first discovered the war within on the sporting field. John was an Ohio High School state champion in Track and Field in 1998, and went on to the University of Findlay, where he became the 2002 NCAA All-Ohio indoor track champion in the 800m run and a provisional qualifier to the NCAA Division II track and field national championships in the 800m run.

John is very active in his faith and his local Catholic parish. John and his wife Kristin's dedication to the faith earned them the 2011 Centurion Award from the Diocese of Toledo, given for "Outstanding service to their parish." John is a passionate speaker and has been invited to speak at numerous events and parishes. He teaches and speaks on a variety of topics including The Theology of the Body, the Saints, the Church, Mary, The Great Adventure bible study, and his new education program for children and adults, Saints in the Making University (SIMU). He implements the five steps to winning the war within into every topic he speaks on.

John and his wife Kristin currently reside in northwest Ohio with their four children. John is a mobile eye doctor, and he travels to over 40 nursing homes and developmental disability facilities to provide eye care through his business, Mobile Eyes, LLC, which he started in 2007.

To schedule Dr. John to come speak at your event, or to learn more about his mission, email: john@extraordinarymission.com or go online: **www.ExtraordinaryMission.com**

ACKNOWLEDGMENTS

I can't begin to count how many people played a role in making this book a reality over the past several years. It started as a farfetched item on my dream list, and on more than one occasion I gave up on it and pushed it off to the side for many months. There was always somebody who never let me quit and kept me moving forward.

I am forever grateful to…

My God. It never ceases to amaze me how God blesses my life when I muster the courage to follow his quiet nudges, even when he is nudging me in the opposite direction I want to go.

My four beautiful children and wife Kristin, for encouraging me, believing in me, and sacrificing so much to help make my dreams a reality. You have all brought me an unspeakable joy, and you make me want to be a saint.

My mother and brothers for molding me into who I am and guiding me in the right direction my whole life.

Carol Kurvial, Beth Church, and Matt Kettinger for donating their expertise in editing and theology, and **Bret Huntebrinker** for sharing his design and marketing skills.

All my circle of friends who have encouraged me since long before this book was started.

Fr. Randy Giesige, Fr. Tim Kummerer, Fr. Ron Schock, and all those priests and seminarians who have given me spiritual direction.

Matthew Kelly for inspiring me, encouraging me to dream, and giving me an opportunity.

My Father…you were always there for me. You always watched my races with a stopwatch in hand, which held me accountable to do my best. I know you now hold the stopwatch to the race of my life and your prayers give me strength to never give up. I will see you at the finish line.

JOIN THE CAUSE

Offer your next race to cure cancer...of the soul.

Many people run marathons, half marathons, or 5K's to raise money for cancer research. This is a great idea, we all know too well the devastation bodily cancer can cause. However, Dr. John, and anyone who is willing to accept the challenge, is running races and offering up each mile to raise money for a different type of cancer...cancer of the soul. The greatest diseases of our age are social diseases such as hedonism, individualism, minimalism, indifference, apathy, and moral relativism. The Catholic Church has the antidote to these horrible diseases, but the church is a sleeping giant. We need to wake her up...

Dynamic Catholic is building a world class Confirmation program based on two years of comprehensive research revealing what will reengage disengaged Catholics. This program will be offered for free to every parish in the country... This year alone, Dynamic Catholic is giving away over a million copies of bestselling Catholic books for $2 or $3 a copy. Those are game changers that will turn the tide on Catholicism in America.

You can help by making a pledge for one of Dr. John's races or offering up a race of your own to help Dynamic Catholic or another great Catholic Charity close to your heart. You can accomplish a dream, receive free training and fundraising advice from Dr. John, make a worthy sacrifice for your friends and family....and help save souls!

To learn more and join the cause, visit: **www.ExtraordinaryMission.com**

> *"A race is a war within. The purpose is not to just*
> *finish the race. The purpose is to finish with nothing left to give.*
> *The same is true about life."* -John R. Wood

Notes

1. Cardinal Karol Wojtyla, address at the Eucharistic Congress in Philadelphia (1976).

2. Census of the 2011 Annuario Pontificio (Pontifical Yearbook).

3. Pope John Paul II's "Letter to the Youth of the World," on the topic of vocation, March 31, 1985.

4. C. S. Lewis, *Letters To Malcom: Chiefly on Prayer* (New York: Mariner Books, 2002), 108–109.

5. http://www.ignatiusinsight.com/features2005/colson_satan_aug2005.asp

6. http://www.nimh.nih.gov/health/publications/suicide-in-the-us-statistics-and-prevention/index.shtml

7. The Marist Institute for Public Opinion in Poughkeepsie, N.Y., conducted the survey Dec. 23, 2009–Jan. 4, 2010, among 2,243 Americans, including an oversample of 1,006 "millennials" (those age 18–29). Reported in the Catholic Chronicle Feb. 28, 2010.

8. *The Independent Chronicle,* September 26, 1796.

9. Associated Press, "University of Illinois Instructor Fired Over Catholic Beliefs," July 9, 2010.

10. http://www.fda.gov/BiologicsBloodVaccines/BloodBloodProducts/QuestionsaboutBlood/ucm108186.htm

11. P. Cameron, W. L. Playfair, and S. Wellum, "The Longevity of Homosexuals: Before and After the AIDS Epidemic," Omega: Journal of Death and Dying 29, no. 3 (1994).

12. http://www.catholic.com/tracts/birth-control

13. *Words from God* (Beacon, 1993).

14. *In epistulam Ioannis ad Parthos*

15. McKinley, James C. Jr., "Sports Psychology; It Isn't Just a Game: Clues to to Avid Rooting," *The New York Times,* August 11, 2001.

16. The National Survey on Drug Use and Health Report (NSDUH), "Depression Among Adults Employed Full-Time, by Occupational Category," October, 11, 2007.

17. Matthew Kelly, *The Rhythm of Life: Living Every Day with Passion and Purpose* (New York: Fireside, 1999), 51.

18. Saint Therese of Lisieux, *The Autobiography of Saint Therese of Lisieux: The Story of a Soul* (New York: Doubleday, 2001), 113.

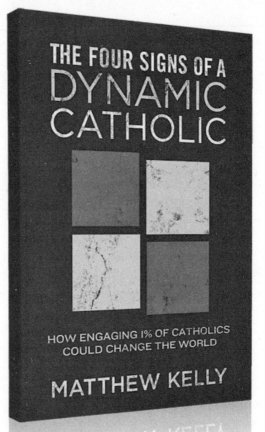